HOW TO BE A
RUBBER BAND

A Formula for Living Resilience Every Day

Erik E. Morales, PhD

Illustrated By Tami Morales

For Mom, Pop, and Tami…Thank you!

CONTENTS

INTRODUCTION

"Well, seeing as the doctor said my immune system
did most of the work,
I believe a discount is in order."

L et's do a little experiment. I want you to pick up the nearest sharp
object within reach—that scissor over there will do—and cut one of
your fingers slightly until it bleeds.

Wait! Don't actually do it, just *imagine* you did. OK…now, do you need to rush to the emergency room and have surgery? Unless you're a hemophiliac, you probably don't.

As you most likely learned in biology class at some point, your body has a built-in series of elaborate and effective self-healing mechanisms that will eventually repair that cut finger and a host of other ailments.

Let's take a deeper look at your cut and what would actually happen. Once the blood vessels under the skin are torn, blood will begin to secrete. At the risk of stating the obvious, this is not a good thing. Like the Cuban government, your body does not want its residents to leave. In this case your blood is like a group of refugees trying to escape to Florida. And just as a few dissidents on a rickety raft would not be the end of the Castro regime, a bit of blood loss would not be the end of you. But too much and, *Havana, we have a problem!* So immediately your body sends blood platelets to the site of the wound. These platelets stick together and clot, thus plugging up the fissure. Soon after, a protective scab begins to form over the wound, allowing the skin cells underneath the time they need to begin regenerating. To make certain there is not an infection, white blood cells attack any germs that may have found their way into the wound. Once the skins cells have done their thing, the scab falls off to reveal the shiny new skin below.

As amazing as this is, thankfully this is not our only built-in system of self-protection. You have an immune system that is on constant red alert throughout your body, monitoring your health and responding quickly to invaders. To accomplish this, your body identifies the particular makeup of the intruders and releases antibodies specifically designed to thwart their attacks. These antibodies are so clever, so durable, that even after the conflict has been resolved, they retain the ability to fight off that infection should it ever return. In fact, paradoxically, the successful defeat of any particular intruders can actually *increase* our ability to fight them off the next time, which ultimately improves our overall health. We can build up a resistance to those specific strains, thus *immunizing ourselves.* In the end we can emerge stronger than before the initial trauma.

The full potential of our bodies to heal themselves is far from having been fully realized. Each day we are discovering more and more about the body's remarkable ability to actively aid in its own healing processes, thus expanding the boundaries of possibility. As just one example, we are only now beginning to understand how stem cells can be used to regrow essential organs that have been damaged or diseased. What was science fiction a few short decades ago is now simply *science.* Just think what the next twenty years will bring.

Probably the best part of our amazing, self-generating, protective systems is that (thank goodness) we don't have to understand them, guide them, or tell them what to do. Like GPS, cell phones, and virtually all of the technology we now use on a daily basis, we don't need to understand our systems in order to benefit from their magic.

Think about all the physical ailments we have that, with little or no conscious effort from us, will eventually heal themselves: Most headaches go away in a few hours. Sore throats and colds last only a day or two. And most fractured bones eventually heal on their own. Though it is tempting, it behooves us to resist taking this for granted. Imagine if for our bodies and healing mechanisms to work, we actually had to understand *how* they worked? Given the state of science and biology education, in the United States at least, most of us would be in a virtually endless amount of chronic pain and total disability.

As touched upon above, it appears our autoimmune systems have an ironic bent to them, given that often the effort and energies used to heal a trauma make us that much stronger and thus better prepared should that or a similar trauma return.

This reminds me of something my seventh grade industrial arts teacher, Mr. Lashefski, showed us decades ago that still sticks with me today.

We were working with wood, making birdhouses we were supposed to give our mothers for Mother's Day (apparently the early 1980s experienced a massive homeless bird epidemic for we seemed to do this every year). A classmate's piece of wood split in two accidentally while he was hammering a nail into it. And even though the kid was in seventh grade, he started crying like a baby (I remember my seventh grade brain thinking, *Man, this kid must really love birdhouses!*).

I remember Mr. Lashefski putting glue on one edge of the broken piece of wood and joining it to the other edge then placing the newly adjoined pieces into a steel vice. He turned the handle of the vice gradually until the glued pieces were held firmly together. It is what he said next that stood out most in my mind.

In an ever-so-slight Polish accent, he proclaimed, "Once these two pieces have had time to dry, the splintered part that was joined together with the glue will actually be the *strongest* part of the entire piece of wood." This blew my seventh grade mind. How could a part that was so badly splintered just minutes ago become the *strongest*? It didn't make sense then, but it does now. This was an early introduction to the wonder of resilience—when and where we break can provide us with unique opportunities to emerge as strong or even stronger.

Limits of Natural Resilience

So how does all this help inform our thinking about resilience?

First, let's affirm and celebrate that we are literally *built* to be resilient—to bounce back from a myriad of assaults, to consistently regain and regenerate our health. The complex systems of protection and immunity are core parts of who we are not ancillary, postproduction "add-ons."

So much so that we don't even need to think about them in order for them to work. They are us at a very basic cellular level. So whether you believe in evolution, Adam and Eve, or intelligent design, or you believe we descended from a now extinct race of martian squirrels, one thing for certain is that we were constructed, from the inside out, to be resilient.

Second, as amazingly elegant, effective, and involuntary as our self-protective mechanisms often are, even with medical science moving at such a rapid pace, their reach is limited. For every disorder that eventually fixes itself, there are ten that without conscious intervention would debilitate the quality of our lives and/or eventually kill us. So while we are grateful for these built-in shields, we must do all that *we* can to bolster and increase their sturdiness and capacity for protection. A broken ankle may indeed heal itself, but a trip to an orthopedic surgeon will not only increase the likelihood of healing but also help ensure less lasting damage. Yes, we should value and appreciate the gift of our natural proclivity for resilience, but we also have a *responsibility* to *actively* cultivate it.

I have spent virtually my entire adult life exploring and researching resilience and related phenomena. In order to do this, I have immersed myself in various related academic disciplines including psychology, anthropology, sociology, economics, and history. However, even with all of these sincere efforts, I am still consistently surprised and humbled by what I learn (and realize I don't know). Each person, each challenge, and each response opens up new possibilities as to what causes and contributes to individual resilience in a complex world.

Thankfully, as idiosyncratic as the resilience process sometimes feels, several shared overarching themes have emerged. While these concepts often manifest themselves in unique ways (depending on the specific challenge an individual may be facing), in general they are evident across ethnic, socioeconomic, age, and gender lines.

A Well-Built Rubber Band

An umbrella theme, which will be a leitmotif of our journey, is the simple yet profound concept of stretching, and our *metaphorical paradigm* (a phrase that is neither simple nor particularly profound) will be that of the well-built rubber band. Conscious or not, resilient people exhibit the flexibility to both adapt to and *encompass* their challenges while retaining the strength of elasticity to return to form once the crisis has been resolved. To briefly plagiarize myself (Is it technically plagiarizing if you steal from yourself?) from the next chapter, "Prior to dealing with a particular stressor, this person's band is in its original, wholesome, contented shape. Once the individual engages with the problem, the band is stretched as wide as is necessary to endure. It can stretch and stretch if need be. As long as it is not stretched beyond its limit, the band can accommodate most any challenge. Once the stressor is over, the band will return, more or less, back to its original shape." So how does one build oneself up to this degree? Fortunately, at least some of the answers are outlined in this work.

A Formula for Resilience

In addition to our rubber band metaphor, a tool that is helpful in conceptualizing the resilience process (and which serves as this book's format) is the following original resilience formula:

$$R = A + M + Ac$$

$$\text{Resilience} = \text{Acceptance} + \text{Meaning} + \text{Action}$$

This formula was not so much created as revealed. Resulting from a thorough review of the research literature, conducting original research, and general observation—like a cake when it is ready to come out of the oven, these themes and their interconnectedness just kept rising to the top. And while the formula is admittedly an oversimplification (as would be any formula attempting to capture such an incomprehensibly wide array of experiences), based on my research and observations, the resilience process follows this general blueprint to a surprising degree.

Directly below is a brief look at each variable. This will be followed by much deeper analysis and exploration.

Acceptance

Acceptance refers to *undiluted* recognition and affirmation of what has occurred without the need to change the immutable aspects of the event and/or its consequences. It's about acquiescing to the extent necessary and fighting the intense desire—bordering on instinct— to engage in delusion, denial, and fantasy. This concept is relatively simple to understand, but it can be exceedingly difficult to live. When trauma occurs we *so* badly want to erase its existence that we will sometimes go to great, though often unhealthy, lengths to achieve this goal. The problem is it's always a losing battle. Unless you're Superman—who, devastated by the death of his beloved Lois Lane, reversed the rotation of the Earth, thus turning back time to before she perished—you will not be able to change the physics of what has occurred.

Meaning

We are using meaning in a broad sense to include *both* our perception of events as well as how important or meaningful something may be to us.

In contrast to acceptance, meaning is our *interpretation* of what the immutable aspects of the event signify to us. While we cannot change what happened, we can *influence* what *what happened* means, which to an extent does change what happened. After you have reread that sentence several times, I hope you'll see that it does make some sense. As we will soon see, we reinterpret like this all the time.

Meaning also refers to how important or valuable something is to us. Using and identifying what is personally meaningful to us can be a source of virtually unlimited energy and motivation. Resilient people recognize this potential and habitually tap into this energy source in order to cultivate the reservoirs of energy necessary to do what is required.

Action

Each of the three variables in the resilience formula is equally important, but, as George Orwell might have put it, some are *more equal* than others. Action is the *sine qua non* of resilience. It involves not only doing (and the motivation to do) but also *how* we determine what we can/should do, as well as our beliefs regarding the efficacy of the specific deed. Here is where strategic thinking, self-efficacy, persistence, and delayed gratification rest their figurative heads. Resilient people employ both their acceptance of whatever the trauma may be and their sense of what it may mean to design action plans they "know" will influence outcomes. And they believe so wholeheartedly in their influence that they keep acting until change occurs.

As important as action is, without healthy acceptance and strategic meaning, all the action in the world can be pointless. An army can have the most powerful guns in the world, but if they are pointed in the wrong direction or lack the right ammunition, what's the use? To carry the metaphor one step further, if action is the gun, meaning provides the ammunition, and acceptance, the target coordinates.

Throughout this text we will explore how these admittedly nebulous and fluid categories of variables can work harmoniously to produce infinite variations of resilience.

Note: The content of this book is based on a combination of original research, a review of the works of others in related fields, and personal observation. Unless explicitly noted all of the illustrations and examples are inspired by real people and their experiences, though names and some of the details have been altered for clarity, brevity, and/or to ensure confidentiality and anonymity.

CHAPTER I:
RESILIENCE 101

"Someone needs to tell the *boulder* it's only a metaphor."

On November 7, 1991, I returned from my job as a high school English teacher to my crowded third-floor walk-up in New York City's East Village to a television on and my roommate's greeting of "Did you hear?" Before the words "Hear what?" left my mouth, my eyes found the color television propped in the corner of our cramped studio apartment. There was Earvin "Magic" Johnson, all six feet nine of him, telling the world that he had been diagnosed with HIV.

At the time HIV/AIDS was not only perceived as a death sentence but was also considered more of a shameful illness than it is today—an illness to be concealed, not announced to the world on ESPN. Furthermore, to put things into a socio-emotional context, at the time it was the potentially realistic threat most people my age feared. We weren't scared of being drafted to fight in Vietnam, nor were we scared of the possibility of a nuclear strike or a terrorist attack—at a visceral level, my generation and I feared HIV/AIDS above all else.

So there on the TV sat this future hall of famer, inarguably among the top ten greatest basketball players ever to lace up sneakers, revealing his nightmare death sentence to the entire world.

If adversity really does reveal character, we were all about to get some revelations into what kind of character Magic really had. He had been known for his smile, for his gregariousness, and for his warmth. We would soon see if those attributes were who he really was or just who he was when things happened to be going well. In all honesty, at that moment, I thought the magic of Magic's contagious smile as well as his renowned zest for life were gone forever, first figuratively, then literally.

But a funny thing happened on the way to the forum, and it continued to unfold over the next twenty years. Magic's smile did not diminish, nor did his enthusiasm or his *joie de vivre*. In fact, if possible, everything about him, *including* his physique, appeared to grow stronger. He did eventually retire from the NBA, but he also became a spokesperson for HIV/AIDS education; created nonprofit community outreach initiatives; expanded his business interests; opened movie theaters in neglected inner-city neighborhoods; became a popular sports commentator; and, as recently as the writing of this sentence, spearheaded a group purchasing the Los Angeles Dodgers baseball team.

Over the course of two decades, he has taken massive action to fight his HIV. In addition to seeking out the most highly regarded specialists in the field, he works-out like a madman, eats right, and takes potent cocktails of various medications. His efforts continue to pay off, so much so that to the shock of almost everyone, he has all but beaten the HIV virus, and there is virtually no sign of it left in him.

Perhaps the most amazing part of his journey, and the part most relevant to our discussion here, is that when we see Magic on television now, we don't see "HIV," we don't see "AIDS," and we don't see illness. We see Magic.

What makes him truly resilient is not that he simply *survived* (though that is impressive in and of itself) but that he endured his challenges *without losing himself in the process*. He stretched and he grew, but he retained his sense of self, his essence. If he had "beaten" HIV but become a bitter recluse in the process, then he would have been a *survivor* but not necessarily *resilient*. Resilience means enduring the stress while maintaining, to the extent possible, a prestress sense of self.

And exactly how did Magic live resilience? I have not interviewed him, nor do I have access to any secret files, but based on what I have researched, this is what I see.

At first there was shock, denial, anger, and disbelief— a figurative blindsiding by a silent but devastating Mack truck. But eventually he accepted that which was immutable: he had tested positive for HIV.

But here is the extraordinary part: that was the only ground he was willing to give. It was a test for a particular virus, and it was positive. That was it. I can only imagine how difficult it must have been to refrain from adding more to the mix—to lash out at circumstance; to bathe oneself in shame, self-loathing, and paralyzing fear; to shake a fist at the world and scream, "Why me?"

The significance of his acceptance can only be fully appreciated when we look at how he did, and didn't, interpret what that positive test *meant*. When it came to meaning, he assumed almost complete control. The test did not mean that he was going to die any time soon or that he had sinned against God. It did not mean that he was being singled out for punishment or that he had done something to deserve it. It did not mean that he would become a hermit or that he had to live in shame and hide his condition. All it meant was that he had the human immunodeficiency virus within him, and as with any virus—be it chicken pox, bronchitis, or even the common cold—how destructive it may turn out to be was in large part up to him. Even in a potentially traumatic physical and emotional context, he interpreted, not only rationally but also equally as important, in his own best interest. Tough, I know, but ultimately a prerequisite to resilience.

Why was Magic able to eschew much of the stigma that usually comes with HIV? Because unlike the positive test itself, the stigma was not immutable, nor was it absolute. Because he had the choice to dismiss it, he could. As we will see, the distinction between acceptance and meaning often boils down to immutability. Resilient people only accept that which they absolutely must—everything else is fair game for self-interested interpretation.

Magic's decisions about what HIV meant (and didn't mean) buoyed him and helped procure the energy needed to take massive action. He proceeded to gather relevant and reputable information and resources and persistently acted on their basis and guidance. The meds, the exercise regimen, and the positive attitude all flowed from how he interpreted the trauma and collectively cultivated his ultimate resilience.

What We Really Mean by Resilience

Resilience does not just mean achieving (though achievement may be an outcome), nor does it simply mean surviving (I can survive a mugging, but if I am forever terrified of strangers, and my agoraphobia grows to the point that I never leave my house, am I really resilient?). Resilience is about *enduring* challenges without losing who we are—our senses of individuality, our "individual essences" for lack of a better term.

Resilience means maintaining our original selves despite consistent collisions with our world's stressors. It means seeing ourselves through the storm and coming out the other side as dry as we were before. This does not mean we will be exactly the same after the storm, but our core selves will remain intact.

Genesis of an Idea

There are two critical life events that have given birth to my fascination with overcoming life's obstacles and living resilience. The first helped define my childhood and created early gratitude for the concept. The second brought me to the empirical research already done on the topic, as well as the cultivation of my own extensive inquiry.

To begin we'll go back in time to an exotic location.

My father was born in 1922 in a small village in a small country on a small island in the Caribbean. To say he was poor is like saying Bill Gates is "well-off." Meat (usually rabbit) was served once a month, if they were lucky, with bland soup and the occasional fried plantain, making up the rest of their food pyramid. According to my father, hunger was something he and his siblings lived with but never really got used to.

⌒

The island was Hispaniola, home to two countries, one more impoverished than the other. And while my father was lucky enough to be born on the "wealthier" Dominican side, at the time this was small consolation.

With about twelve brothers and sisters who needed to be fed at any given point (I say *about* because several died during childhood or at birth), his single, working mother did what she could. The family survived by selling homemade *dulces* (candies) and fresh cut flowers grown in the backyard garden. When sales quotas were not met, Mama simply added more water to the soup.

As if this were not enough, when he was ten, my father became the victim of a typhoid fever epidemic that swept across the island. At the time and in his community, this highly infectious disease was lethal more often than not. His mother quarantined him in the only room with a door, letting him sweat out the fever and hoping against hope for recovery.

As my father lay there, coming in and out of fever dreams, he overheard the priest tell his mother to order the coffin soon to make certain he would receive a "proper Christian burial." A day later he overheard the doctor (who would not actually walk *into* the room for fear of contracting the dreaded disease) say that *if* my father managed to ride out the illness and hold on for a month, he would survive but that it was very unlikely.

The next morning my father grabbed a small stone and scraped a chalk line on the concrete wall next to his bed. He promised himself that no matter what, he would do this every morning. He convinced himself that he would eventually make thirty lines, survive the month, and ultimately live. After all, that's what the doctor, the most respected person in the community, said, right?

Each evening, he went to sleep in pools of sweat, battling the persistent fear that the next day would never come. But each morning he woke to the roosters and the hot Caribbean sun and morsels of gratitude. He'd then reach under his bed for his rock and scrape another line. A week passed, then two; the scratched lines, in groups of five, on the wall began adding up—a primitive tableau, marking time and generating hope.

According to my father, on the morning of the thirtieth day, when he drew the fifth line across the sixth group of five, he got to his feet, walked out the door, and pronounced himself all better, *"Siento mejor ahora!"*

And better he was. That fall he began school for the first time, his mother finally having the money to buy the required clothing and shoes. And fueled with the vow that his future family would *never*, no matter what, feel the hunger he had been forced to live with, my father attacked school with a ferocity and tenacity that bordered on obsession. "A" after "A," scholarship after scholarship, degree after degree, he made his way to the United States in the 1950s with a medical degree and an unquenchable desire for a level of comfort and security that simply could not have been acquired on a Caribbean island ruled by a ruthless, power-hungry dictator.

Fast-forward about forty years to a very different locale over a thousand miles away from that small, tropical island: a crowded high school cafeteria in the Bronx, New York. There I stood watch, a twenty-one-year-old sentinel and recent graduate of New York University's English Education Teacher-Certification program. It would be here, in this unlikeliest of places, where the second critical life event inspiring my exploration of resilience would unfold.

I found myself on that most dreaded of teacher obligations—cafeteria duty—surveying hordes of high school students downing Tater Tots and rectangular pizzas off Styrofoam lunch trays. I had been at that school for a few months and was still coming to grips with the vast and depressing array of obstacles that these kids (it is difficult to write *kids* when most of them were bigger than I was, and almost as old) faced every day. That ugly list of urban maladies that still persists today was alive and thriving in early 1990s South Bronx: rampant drug use and dealing, teenage motherhood, absent fatherhood, ubiquitous violence, police brutality, underfunded community resources, institutional racism, and on and on.

So as I kept an eye out for both food fights and fistfights, I noticed a young male student sitting by himself reading what I assumed was a comic book. He didn't look any different from the other students, but it was rare to see *any* student reading *anything*, even a comic. I wandered over to him nonchalantly and glanced over his shoulder, expecting to see *The Amazing Spider-Man* or *Mad Magazine*. To my utter shock, I saw the stark-black letters of *The New Yorker* masthead.

Now, remember the context here; seeing a kid reading *The New Yorker* in this lunchroom was like seeing Donald Trump with a bullhorn spearheading an Occupy Wall Street protest. Yes, it was unusual, but it also elicited a sense of hope and optimism.

I did some reconnaissance about the boy and got some interesting intel. Most relevant to our discussion was that while his home life and upbringing were not, at least on the surface, substantively different from many of the other students, this kid was on his way to Princeton with an almost full academic scholarship. Pretty amazing stuff. All I could think was, how and why did this happen?

That year I taught five sections of eleventh- and twelfth-grade English, and my rosters averaged thirty-seven students per class. Unfortunately (or fortunately depending on how you looked at it), on average only twenty of the thirty-seven students actually showed up to class on a regular basis. At the end of the year, of my sixty-two seniors, ten were college-bound. Of these, six went to community colleges in the borough, two to state universities in the northern part of the state, and two to moderately selective private colleges. The following year the unofficial word around town indicated that all but three had dropped out of college. The "survivors" included one from the moderately selective private college and two from the community colleges. And while we can question why so many did not make it, I was more interested in those who did.

The question of why and how such anomalies occurred stayed with me and eventually become the topic of my doctoral dissertation eight years later back at NYU. My specific focus was on what I discovered had been termed "academic resilience" (exceptional academic achievement despite severe psychosocial-economic stressors), but through this process I was forced to immerse myself in all of the resilience research, beginning with its foundation—emotional/personal resilience (eventual *emotional* well-being despite severe psychosocial stressors).

In the end I came to the conclusion that the ingredients of various forms of resilience crossover to a large extent, and that people can learn a great deal from understanding the resilience of others. And, perhaps most importantly, I am certain that if they are willing to focus their energies in specific ways, people can indeed *cultivate* resilience in their own lives.

Resilience Research

Years of research on how students, like the avid reader from the Bronx, ended up seventy miles and worlds away at Princeton resulted in an Academic Resilience Cycle (see figure one below).

The Resilience Cycle includes a "hub" and five "spokes" (aka steps) representing the educational resilience process as demonstrated by the participants. The theory is cyclical in that its progression tends to repeat itself as students enter new academic phases in their lives and face the accompanying challenges. Furthermore, it is helpful to note that resilience theory in general operates under the assumption that individuals coming from difficult or stressful environments can succeed if they (a) have access to valuable protective factors and (b) exploit them.

The five spokes are:

Spoke 1: The student realistically recognizes her or his major risk factors.

Spoke 2: The student manifests and/or seeks out protective factors that have the potential to offset or mitigate negative effects of the risk factors.

Spoke 3: The student manages her or his protective factors in concert to propel herself or himself toward high academic achievement.

Spoke 4: The student recognizes the effectiveness of the protective factors and continues to refine and implement them.

Spoke 5: The constant and continuous refinement and implementation of protective factors, along with the evolving vision of the student's desired destination, sustain the student's progress.

The Hub: Consists of "Emotional Intelligence" and the effective and purposeful management of emotions.

If we speak of the steps of the cycle as spokes, then there is a "hub" around which the spokes rotate and gain momentum. This hub is an amalgam of closely related self-management abilities, including skillful and effective management of emotions amid stressful times, adeptness in social environments, impulse control, and effective decision making under duress. The combined articulation of these basic characteristics can be found in the concept of *emotional intelligence,* popularized by Daniel Goleman[1] and about which we will discuss in greater detail later in this text.

This "Hub" also closely reflects what Paul Tough in his book *How Children Succeed: Grit, Curiosity, and the Hidden Power of Character*[2] refers to as "executive function" and which he describes as among the most significant indicators of future success. According to Tough executive function is a collection of higher-order mental abilities that enable people to manage their emotions and deal with stress. While Tough goes into the physiology of the brain and how chronic stress can impair our executive functions, relevant to our discussion is the essential role it plays as a facilitator of resilience. Ultimately, emotional intelligence and executive function allow effective utilization of whatever protective factors may be available.

Figure 1. The Resilience Cycle, Morales 2008

Overall, the research regarding resilience was born from a simple yet incredibly profound observation. An observation that many of us have probably made at one point or another: no matter how apparently painful and virulent the stressors faced by a group of individuals may be, not every member of that group succumbs to the usual deleterious effects of those stressors. In other words not *every* girl who is abandoned by her father grows up to make poor choices in men, not *every* boy who is abused contemplates suicide as an adult, not *every* child growing up in abject poverty drops out of high school, and not *every* person diagnosed with a malignant cancer crawls into an emotional fetal position and waits to die. There are anomalies, always. Depending on the particular study and stressors being looked at, usually between 10 and 20 percent of potential "victims" prove resilient.

There are several different types of resilience studies that make up the resilience literature. Originally, psychosocial resilience was the most common type studied (the work of Garmenzy, 1991[3]; Rutter, 1979[4]; and Werner & Smith, 1992[5] are seminal in this field). This involved studying samples of individuals who had been exposed to psychological stressors (e.g., poverty, alcoholic or schizophrenic parents, etc.) who then grew into "well-adjusted" adults. Later, as exemplified above, educational researchers began looking at statistically at-risk students (those who, based on their demographic backgrounds, were *supposed* to fail) who ended up doing exceptionally well in school. All of these researchers found that regardless of the severity of the stressors that afflicted a given population, resilient individuals emerged. This begged two questions—*why* and *how?*

Focusing on these questions represents a monumental shift in thinking. A shift that has been reflected in part by the plethora of recent works exploring what can be broadly termed "positive psychology." Work by researchers/ authors Daniel Gilbert,[6] Martin Seligman,[7] Christopher Peterson,[8] and Carol Dwek[9] has asked that we broaden the target of psychology and personal development to better understand the variables that both correlate with and cause happiness, fulfillment, and quality of life.

The psychological and research establishment is now applying rigorous scientific method to an area that has long been the province of less rigorous, but often equally influential, authors whose work can be found in the seemingly ever expanding "self-help" sections of your local bookstores. From Napolean Hill in 1937 to Tony Robbins today, as a culture we have long been intrigued by how and why some people succeed and others don't.

Interestingly, the change in emphasis engendered by the resilience model—from failure to success—mirrors to a certain extent model shifts in healthcare as well. Until recently it was relatively rare to hear terms like "wellness" and "preventative health" in the medical lexicon. However, more and more medical researchers are now studying health in order to promote it.

Even those tightfisted, bottom-line folks at medical insurance companies have begun buying into the value of prevention and wellness—putting their money where their mouths are, many of these companies will actually reimburse their clients' gym memberships!

Cleary the time is right to apply this shift in thinking to our own lives on a broader level and to embrace resilience as both a daily and lifelong pursuit. Consequently, the goal here is to explore and present ideas about resilience in ways that combine the rigorous data-driven nature of empirical researcher with the user-friendly, inspirational, and pragmatic ethos of the self-help gang.

What Resilience Is Not

According to most film historians, *Citizen Kane* is among the greatest, if not *the* greatest, films ever made. For anybody not familiar with the basic plot, the film chronicles the life and career of newspaper magnate Charles Foster Kane. While Kane manages to acquire unparalleled wealth and power (successful by most standards), he ends up bitter, miserable, and alone, longing for the innocence of his youth symbolized by his childhood sled, "Rosebud." Granted, this brief synopsis is an oversimplification of a complex story; however, it is enough to pose the question, was Charles Foster Kane resilient? I posit that he was not. While he achieved a great deal and did exhibit extraordinary ambition and persistence, the price he paid (the innocence and wonder of his youth) was ultimately too high.

The literary and film worlds are filled with similar themes of Faustian bargains, where protagonists literally and figuratively sell their souls for what they think they want only to find out, like Kane, that the price was too high. Examples range from the sublime (e.g., the devil attempts to contaminate Job's soul in The Book of Job from the Old Testament of the Bible) to the ridiculous (e.g., Homer Simpson sells his soul for a doughnut). Our concept of resilience eschews this catch-22 and posits that we can both endure and achieve while retaining our fundamental and essential natures.

Resilience Big and Small

Another common misconception is that the resilient journey must be a grand epic of loss, pain, near death, and ultimate resurrection. We may sometimes believe that because we have smartphones and organic supermarkets and central air conditioning, we cannot truly be resilient. A common anxiety in children of the Great Depression that began in the late 1920s revolves around their feelings of never being able to match their parents' grit, persistence, and ultimate successes. No matter what they do, they know their parents had it tougher, and, therefore, "winning" is impossible for them.

I have experienced this very conundrum in relation to my father's story presented earlier. I grew up listening to detailed renderings of the abject poverty he overcame and was often expected to feel guilty for having it "easy"—like it was *my* fault I had shoes and clothes and cable TV. There is an ongoing joke in my family that gets revisited every summer. When I was nine or ten years old, my father asked if I wanted some ice cream. I replied, "What kind?" At that he launched into an animated diatribe about how when he was a child, no youngster would *dare* ask "What kind?" if offered so rare a luxury as ice cream.

To this day at family gatherings when ice cream is offered, somebody will inevitably shout "What kind?" and we'll all laugh. I don't think my father meant to diminish any sense of personal accomplishment I might feel, but the fact is I did (and still do to an extent) downplay anything I achieved because I felt it could in no way measure up to his exploits. And while it's easy to *say,* "Well, you *shouldn't* be in competition with your parents," it is a natural human tendency to compare one's own accomplishments with those from your clan who came before.

We may all long to be the next Nelson Mandela, but, thank goodness, most of us will never face twenty-seven years of unjust imprisonment only to come out with a desire to unite those who imprisoned us with the rest of our country. For every Mandela there are millions of people who have lost loved ones to cancer. For every Viktor Frankl (holocaust survivor and activist whom we will get to know better later), there are millions of children who experience their parents' sudden divorce, and for every Harriet Tubman risking her freedom to provide safe passage for hundreds of runaway slaves, there are millions of people struggling to overcome various forms of addiction.

Personal challenges, like ideal dress sizes and good incomes, are individual and relative. So don't feel bad if you have no massive psychosocial-emotional baggage. Be grateful! And don't cheapen the challenges you do have. Too often we minimize our own struggles, which can lead to underestimating what it may take to overcome them. The bottom line is that your problems are your problems, and they don't have to be enormous to be significant.

Caveat

I do not know how people *should* react to the myriad of calamities they may face. I cannot and will not tell someone who has had a devastating personal loss what to do or how to feel. But studying and sharing what others have done and how others have responded can shed a nourishing light on what is possible.

Finally, please note that this book and the ideas presented are not a substitute for the services of mental health or other professionals. If you have a serious, chronic psychological malady and/or have survived severe physical and/or emotional abuse, please reach out for help. However, do use this text and the ideas herein as a complement to your courageous journey.

Personalizing Resilience: Perry's Story

None of the ideas presented here, or in the resilience formula, mean anything outside of the messy, unscripted, and often volatile place we call "the real world." So let's take a look at how these concepts can play out there.

When I was a junior at New York University in the early 1990s, I had a fraternity brother and friend we'll call Perry. Perry was, and is, a pretty amazing guy, though upon looking at him, nothing extraordinary immediately pops out. But if you got to know him, you'd begin to realize that he lives resilience in almost everything he does. He is a particularly strong illustration of the value and importance of self-efficacy as well as of how sustaining a deep sense of sincere meaning can be.

Perry never cured cancer, endured false imprisonment, or won the Nobel Peace Prize, but he exhibited the sort of everyday resilience that is within the reach of all of us. The following narrative of his law school odyssey demonstrates how the ideas and concepts discussed earlier can facilitate resilience within a real-world context.

Ever since his freshman year of college, Perry had two dreams: to go to law school at the prestigious University of Texas at Austin and to become a skilled attorney. Having visited the state a few years earlier to attend a large music festival, he fell in love with Texas—the wide open spaces, the people, and especially country music—and dreamed of living and studying law in the Lone Star State.

Perry's passion for country music was evidenced by his extensive collection of rare country and western records that he played *constantly*, to the dismay and annoyance of his fraternity brothers' ears. In our fraternity house, it was often Merle Haggard and Lyle Lovett versus Salt-N-Pepa and Vanilla Ice (Hey, it was the early '90s!).

So after taking the LSATs during his junior year, he mailed in his application for early admission and confidently awaited good news. After all he was an excellent student, had worked hard, and was used to getting what he had worked for.

A month or so later, a thin envelope arrived at our fraternity house addressed to him with a University of Texas logo and return address in the upper left-hand corner. Now, anyone who has ever applied to college probably knows that a *thin* envelope is rarely a good thing. Most of the time it is a brief, automated statement reading something along the lines of, "We regret to inform you that…blah, blah, blah…" This contrasts greatly with acceptance letters that usually come in thick packets containing detailed information, forms to sign, and other materials to send back. Well, we all knew what Perry's dream was, and even though it was a thin envelope, we remained hopeful and eagerly watched him open it. But as expected it was one of those cold and heartless rejection letters.

We tried to console him. One guy said, "I guess it wasn't meant to be. There are other good law schools." And another said, "Everything happens for a reason. Maybe you weren't *meant* to go to Texas." A third said, "Look on the bright side: at least you won't have to miss out on

New York pizza." While it was disappointing, Perry accepted his lack of acceptance. The letter was real, not a mistake and not a bad dream—but also not the end of the story. Many people would have stopped there. He gave it his best shot, and it didn't work out. C'est la vie! But Perry is not most people.

One of the ways he responded was by asking himself what the letter *meant*. This is where many people would have been stopped dead in their tracks. It is the *interpretation* of the event, in this case the letter, that would either close the door completely or leave it open and pregnant with possibility. Many would allow insecurity and self-doubt to infuse their interpretation with pessimism. However, Perry's modus operandi was much more consistent with self-efficacy and opportunity rather than with impotence and defeatism. So he crafted an interpretation that was both true *and* in his own best interest. For Perry all the letter meant was that the collection of papers referred to as an "application" he had mailed-in months earlier did not, at that particular moment, warrant his admission. That's it. The letter did not mean he was not good enough, nor did it mean that a future version of his application would not be good enough. For Perry the letter was a comma, not a period.

Perry had an extraordinary ability to both see and accept the reality of what was happening at any given point and focus only on the variables over which he had control. Many would have, understandably so, gotten caught-up in the emotions of the moment—the disappointment, the frustration, the embarrassment at having failed at a goal that was made public. All of this would have caused many of us to take the easy way out and turn acceptance of a rejection letter into acceptance of defeat, if for no other reason than to limit the emotional distress. We may have even convinced ourselves that it simply wasn't meant to be and acknowledged that it was not too late to apply to other schools. But as I said earlier, Perry was different. He did not allow emotions to cloud his approach and was secure enough in himself that a bit of public failure would not significantly inhibit his ambition.

Perry knew that in order to fully understand the situation and strategically move ahead, he needed more information. He could not fully discern the letter's ultimate meaning, its implications, or how to proceed, without more data.

The next morning Perry called the law school admissions office, negotiated his way past several secretaries and administrators, and finally found an assistant dean who, apparently against regulations, would tell him *why* he was not admitted.

"Well," the dean said, "you did have strong grades and a good record, but your LSAT scores were a *bit* low for us. We had an extraordinary crop of applicants this year, and you just didn't make the cut. I'm sorry." There is no doubt this was tough to hear… *You just didn't make the cut*…harsh words indeed. Harsh enough to make most of us profoundly question our overall adequacy as human beings, let alone law school candidates. Though not easy, Perry refused to allow himself to go down this road. He had built enough belief in himself that he would not allow his self-worth to be determined by some guy in a cowboy hat on the other end of a phone two thousand miles away.

Again focusing on what he *could* influence, Perry asked the man if it was too late to retake the LSATs and submit new scores. The man said that would be fine, and with that Perry still had hope.

In planning his next move, Perry had to be strategic. If he just retook the exam without changing anything, then logic and common sense says he would get about the same score and the same end result. Just as with finding out why he was not accepted, he needed insights and knowledge he simply did not possess at that moment. One of his favorite quotes was from Albert Einstein: "We cannot solve problems with the same level of thinking that created them." He knew he had to increase his level of thinking. This prompted him to reach for one of his favorite resources: smart people.

Perry was big on using others. Not in an exploitive sense, but with the idea of taking advantage of the knowledge, expertise, and compassion of those who are in positions to help. Being a kind and affable young man himself, Perry had accumulated a small but prestigious coterie of professors and advisors at NYU he had come to rely on for guidance at various points in his college career.

So he made some phone calls presenting his situation and seeking advice. Curiously, several of the professors he reached out to mentioned the same LSAT preparation course that, though expensive, had an excellent reputation for raising scores. But there was a problem, a $1,000 problem to be exact—$1,000 for the five-weekend course. Neither he nor his parents had that kind of extra money. Between NYU tuition, room and board, and the cost of simply living in New York City, there just wasn't much left.

Here is where the degree of Perry's commitment, how *meaningful* the goal was, was both tested and revealed. Going to law school at Texas mattered to him on a level that almost nothing else, aside from his parents and brother, did. For him, attending a prestigious law school out West meant that not only could he live out his fantasy of being surrounded by the beauty of Texas, its climate, its music, and its history, but also that he would emerge prepared to practice law in an area that was a growing passion of his.

Being born and bred in New York, he had an affinity and fascination with the immigrant experience. Having worked summers in the kitchen of a four-star restaurant in Manhattan, he got to know many of the recent immigrants working there and through daily interaction began seeing them as individuals, rather than faceless masses. Aside from becoming virtually fluent in Spanish, while there he gained a deep appreciation for how hard they worked and the invaluable services they performed despite often being treated as third-class citizens. It was there that his commitment to immigrants' rights had been born. Perry had heard, firsthand, story after story documenting the moral and ethical injustices faced by this population: children being pulled out of public schools, families being separated and torn apart, arrests and detentions without due process, and overall relegation to virtual subhuman status. And what better place to study immigration law than in close proximity to the nearly two thousand-mile United States-Mexico border? So while the price of the prep-course (both literally and figuratively) was high, Perry was resolute. He wasn't sure how, but he would get the money.

Unable to sleep because of the dilemma, he lay awake in our cramped dorm room and went through his options. Though it took some time, he once again relied on his ability to realistically and creatively appraise a situation and tried to focus more on solutions than problems. Finally, with reluctance he acknowledged the only practical solution and was finally able to get some sleep.

The next morning Perry gathered up his beloved record collection in two plastic milk crates, schlepped down to a West Village record shop specializing in rare country music, and sold them all.

Most would have been crushed at having to part with items of such sentimental and monetary value, but Perry saw it as a difficult but necessary step closer to what he wanted even more. Yes, he loved his records, but his goal meant more. And he promised himself that *when* (not if) he became a successful attorney, he would buy them all back, every single one of them.

Once he had the cash in hand, he called the LSAT prep company to register for the next class. There was good news and bad news. The good news was that there was one spot left for the upcoming course; the bad news was that it was in Boston. This was yet another test for Perry, but for him the answer was simple.

Every Saturday morning at three o'clock for the next two months, Perry climbed into his 1984 Honda Civic and drove the five hours up I-95 to Boston. He'd usually drive straight to class, which began at nine on the dot. At five he would drive to a nearby motel, spend the night, and go back to class the next morning from nine to twelve. He'd then drive back to New York where he had to be up and ready for an eight thirty philosophy course on Monday morning. Perry completed this grueling routine five times, and I never heard him utter a word of complaint. Not once.

However, what I did not know at the time, and only found out years later over a few beers at one of our old haunts, was that it had not been nearly as effortless for him as it had seemed. About halfway through the five-week course, he seriously contemplated giving up. He was exhausted by all of the driving and early mornings and by doing both his school and LSAT work. Doubt was also creeping into his usually secure mind. He kept asking himself if this would all be worth it, if it was going to pay off in the end. *I failed to get in before, why should this time be any different?* kept running through his head.

Obviously he did not give up, or I wouldn't be using his story. Decades later I asked him how he managed to keep sane, to keep going. He told me that if it had not been for his older brother (who was a practicing attorney at the time) and his encouragement, advice, and support, Perry would have definitely given up on his dream. Apparently, he and his brother worked out a ritual whereby Perry would call him each Saturday of the LSAT course during the lunch break, again that evening when he returned to his motel room, and once again when he returned to New York City (keep in mind this was before cell phones, so keeping in touch on such a regular basis was no easy task). What did they talk about during all of those calls? The preeminence and essential value of the law? The importance of achieving goals? Strategies for the LSAT? Sometimes, but mostly they talked about their childhood. They relayed funny stories about their parents and neighborhood kids they hadn't seen in years: the time when their first dog, a terrier mix, swallowed their mother's wedding ring, and their father had to dig through the dog's waste to get it; the kid down the street who wore the same engineer's cap every day for three years; the time their father fell off the roof and into the sticker bushes while attempting to clean the gutters; and on and on. They talked about all kinds of shared experiences and memories, laughing constantly, and each and every time Perry got off the phone, he felt reenergized and more ready than ever to see things through.

A month or so later, Perry retook his LSATs, and we all went back to watching the mail. Then one day it came! Another thin envelope. More rejection. We were all upset, all over again. The same well-meaning, but ultimately meaningless, condolences spewed forth. At the time I thought that even Perry would have to give in now and change directions.

But Perry's commitment to his goal and his sincere desire to become the best immigration lawyer possible were stronger than I had thought. Ten minutes after receipt of the letter, Perry was back on the phone with the assistant dean he had spoken to previously.

"Well," the assistant dean began, "your LSAT scores did improve significantly, and you are a very strong applicant, but, you see, we're a state school, and we must reserve the majority of our slots for residents of Texas. Given that you live in New York, we just couldn't make the numbers fit. It's a shame though, because had you been a Texas resident, you probably would have been admitted."

Now that we have gotten to know Perry pretty well, what do you think he did? That's right. He found out that in order to establish residency, one had to live in a state for a year. So he packed up the Honda and headed west.

Perry arrived in Texas knowing no one. He supported himself doing odd jobs and with some financial support from his brother. The following year he reapplied to law school. And as confident and self-assured as he was that this would all pay off in the end, he was still only human, and doubt did creep into his head occasionally.

After several months Perry began meeting the mailman at the door on a daily basis. Phone bills, barbeque and Chinese restaurant menus, letters from family members, and assorted advertisements came regularly. Each time he fingered through his mail and came upon a thin envelope, his heart would skip a beat. He'd quickly grab it, turn it over, and hope it wasn't from the university. It needed to be a hearty, thick packet, not one of those oh-so-cruel thin envelopes.

The months kept passing and still no news.

Then one day Perry watched the mailman coming up the walkway, and, though Perry couldn't be certain, he thought he was smiling a bit more than usual. The mailman handed Perry his mail, just brochures and advertisements, then walked away. But then he stopped, and said, "Oh, yeah, I think this one is yours also," and handed him a thick white package with the rust-colored "University of Texas" logo in the upper left-hand corner.

Not only did Perry go on to attend law school at Texas, but he met his future wife there and ended up having three children with her. He graduated at the top of his class, and after a stint as an assistant district attorney, he began specializing in immigration law back in New York. Oh, yeah…a year or so after returning, Perry spent a rainy Saturday afternoon rummaging through vintage New York City record stores buying up as much of his beloved collection as he could. As of our last contact he was only missing three albums.

Is Perry Exceptional?

I guess that is for you to decide. Clearly he has exhibited an extraordinary tendency to remain focused and act diligently despite setbacks. However, nothing he did or experienced was *unbelievable* in the true sense of the word. I mean, he didn't take a pill that made him invisible and sneak into the admissions office and alter applications. He is just a guy who has cultivated an impressive array of tools that he employs with great skill. Simply put, he is made of thick rubber and able to stretch further than most when necessary, all the time retaining his core self. He does not possess some innate quality that necessarily makes him distinctly different from the rest of us. Consequently, in our own ways, we too can deftly negotiate the tribulations that life presents us with while retaining the best parts of who we are. We can become more and remain who we are. We can stretch.

CHAPTER 2:
ACCEPTANCE

"*My Jeffery, a bad influence!?*"

At 3:46 a.m. Pedro heard a thump outside the bedroom window of his well-kept, four-bedroom suburban home. Illuminated by the porch light, he could see his twenty-year-old son lying facedown in a pool of vomit on the front walkway with his pants down around his ankles, his New York Giants boxer shorts exposed, and he was wearing only one black boot. After registering the pitiful site, Pedro returned to bed and went back to sleep.

He woke again at around eight o'clock and went outside to address his son. "Hey William," he said and gave him a kick in the ribs that was a bit harder than he'd intended. "You still say you don't have a drug problem?" William murmured, "It's all good, Pop. I can handle it."

Even after awaking half naked on his front porch, even after wrapping his Toyota Tercel around a tree, even after missing both his high school prom and graduation, even after being rushed to the hospital after using a bad bag of heroin, even after selling the gold crucifix he stole from his grandmother, and even after his five feet eleven frame dropped to 135 pounds, William still did not have a problem. He either could not or would not accept that which was painfully obvious to all of those around him.

The inherent value of seeing things as close to how they really are as possible is a basic yet profound part of the resilience process. This may seem like a clear-cut and obviously valuable aptitude (and perhaps it is), but it is more rare and impactful than one might think.

Before we can engage in this topic, there are some philosophical, epistemological, and existential stumbling blocks with which we must contend. If we don't, we could end up tripping all over ourselves and getting nowhere:

- *What is the true nature of knowledge?*
- *Are "facts" real?*
- *Is there such thing as absolute reality?*
- *Can we <u>really</u> know anything?*

These are endlessly fascinating questions, but, given our focus and goals, they would probably serve more as sources of distraction than enlightenment. Consequently, for the sake of argument and to move things along, wholly accepting reality from a resilience standpoint means seeing and acknowledging with as much clarity and objectivism as reasonably possible. It means holding not only the sugarcoating and rose-colored glasses but all the "sky is falling" doom and gloom as well.

One of the most common exhortations one hears from self-improvement gurus and pop psychologists alike is, "You create your own reality." A good deal of value can be gleaned from this assertion, but many resilient people would argue with it. At the very least, they would argue that one cannot really "create" reality—except maybe *after* they've accepted portions of it.

To think that reality is created by us implies that we control it, and those of us who have experienced great loss or sorrow know this is simply not the case. However, people still cling to this notion despite the extent to which personal experiences continually provide evidence to the contrary.

In a related vein, I sometimes ask my students if the following statement is true:

"Anything is possible."

Most agree vehemently. I then say snarkily, "Really?... Is it possible for me to leap out of this window right now and begin flying around campus?" They usually laugh and say something like, "You know, within reason."

Just as with anything being possible, creating our own reality is a statement we should ingest figuratively rather than literally. Despite how good it feels to say and think, attempting to convince ourselves we are all-powerful beings can undermine our ability to see and accept reality, and ultimately it greatly inhibits resilience.

As in the old adage of separating the wheat from the chaff, the tricky part here is accepting only that which is absolutely necessary (valuable) and discarding the rest. This is difficult because we don't always know where one ends and the other begins.

Another way to think of this *necessary versus unnecessary* battle royal is to contemplate the difference between what is organically *real* and what we as humans have fabricated. Magic Johnson's positive HIV test was actual (necessary)—it was incontrovertible reality, but the stigma and shame many of us would have feared in his place were fabrications (unnecessary). This is not to say they did not exist, but only that they did not *have* to exist. He had no choice about the results of the test, but he did have a choice as to its implications. But again, it is not always easy to distinguish between the two—as in the old ad for audiocassettes, we must often ask, *Is it live, or is it Memorex?*

Figure two, below, represents the process of healthy acceptance conducive to resilience visually. The bigger circle represents a person's perception of the trauma (the stressor, issue, etc.).

Notice how large it is relative to everything else. Basically it is our mind racing with angst and worry. But only a very small portion of it is the actual and essential truth we must accept (the smaller circle).

Think of this essential truth like your carry-on bag at the airport. It contains *only* your essentials (passport, medication, credit cards, etc.). The rest of the circle is all the additional "stuff" *we* have attached to the event. Think of these items as your checked luggage—stuff you may or may not need depending on a bunch of variables that are as of yet still unknown. Most of us reflexively think we *must* accept the entire circle in order to move on, but that is not the case. All you need is your carry-on, the absolute immutable, stripped-down essence—the rest we can see if we need, and to what extent, once we land.

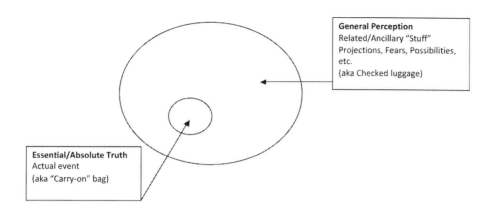

Figure 2 Trauma Perception

The inability (or unwillingness) to see and accept reality, particularly when it hits close to home, keeps many from doing what's necessary to live resilience. This notion jibes well with Rogerian psychotherapies, which emphasize client (as opposed to therapist) centered therapies and the essentialness of acceptance. Carl Rogers himself famously articulated this in what he refers to as his "curious paradox" when he quipped, "When I accept myself just as I am, *then* I can change."

Getting to Know Ourselves: Mirrors and Introspection

The value of perspicacity and objective reasoning is especially relevant, and difficult, when it comes to accurately viewing ourselves. Noted Harvard psychologist Howard Gardner is most famous for his reconceptualizing of what it means to be smart with his well-known *Theory of Multiple Intelligences.*[1] We will further review Gardner's work in our discussion of regeneration activities, but relevant to our discussion here is that he identified *intrapersonal intelligence* as one of seven distinct and vital human intelligences. Gardner believes that those of us highly adept in this intelligence area are not only authentically and keenly aware of ourselves, including our strengths, weaknesses, and emotional trigger points, but rarely engage in *self-deception*.

The absence of this type of self-knowledge and acceptance can be catastrophic. We have probably all observed people who make the same poor decisions over and over again and have the nerve to be surprised *each* and *every* time there is a bad outcome. We see people in relationships that are clearly doomed to fail, but neither member of the couple seems even remotely aware of it. I've successfully predicted several marital separations; one was accurate to the month! I've also met counselors and psychologists who can quickly and accurately diagnose what is ailing the families that come to see them, but appear clueless as to what is going on in their own homes. These are all examples of people who lack high levels of intrapersonal intelligence and frequently miss, or refuse to accept, what is really going on in their own lives.

Evidence for the value and importance of acceptance can also be gleaned from the Twelve Step tradition popularized by Alcoholics Anonymous (AA). Even if you are not an addict, you probably know that the first step is admitting (really *accepting*) that you do have a problem—specifically that you are "powerless over alcohol and that your life has become unmanageable." And while those on the outside can often see the problem with great clarity (as in Pedro and William's case above), those caught in its powerful and potentially devastating grasp seem blind or, even worse, simply deny its existence.

～

In AA it is this first step that receives most of the attention, but subsequent steps demand acceptance as well. What is "searching and fearless inventory" (step four) if not a journey toward painful admissions? Step five follows with a demand that we *admit* to both ourselves and others (as well as God) all of our transgressions. Step nine exhorts us to follow up our admissions with amends for those whom we may have harmed. For many recovering addicts (extant examples of living resilience daily), these admissions serve as the foundation of their recovery. If this accepting were done perfunctorily or insincerely, then like a house built on shifting and shallow sands, the subsequent work and results would be wobbly and weak.

The reality we may have difficulty fully accepting is not always negative. Sometimes we refuse to see or accept things that most would deem positive. However, this lack of acceptance can be just as troubling.

When you look in the mirror or at a picture of yourself, do you see what others see? Probably not. We tend to look at ourselves much differently (and usually more critically) than we look at others. According to researchers a primary reason we find it all but impossible to see ourselves the way others do is the vastly different amounts of data we have regarding ourselves as compared to others. According to Princeton University psychologist Emily Pronin,[2] when we look at others, we interpret using only what we can see on the surface, but when we see ourselves, we filter what we see through all that we know about our inner worlds. As Pronin puts it, "People see themselves differently from how they see others. They are immersed in their own sensations, emotions, and cognitions at the same time that their experience of others is dominated by what can be observed externally." Because we think we know so much about ourselves, our view of ourselves becomes contaminated in a way that our view of others often does not.

The differences in perspective often make us view ourselves more severely and harshly than others. Consequently, we are willing to accept the reality of others more readily than the reality of ourselves. Sometimes we look at ourselves but cannot see that which seems obvious to others. This can happen on a psycho-emotional level (as in William's case) or, perhaps more curiously, on a physical one.

Body dysmorphic disorder is a condition in which the individual literally sees herself (it is usually a she) differently than she actually is. Often these people are by all objective indicators not overweight in the least, but they simply do not see it that way. In part due to deep-seated preoccupations with idealized beauty, feelings of inadequacy, and a longing for control, they appear unable to view and accept an objective picture of themselves.

In a study reviewing fifty cases of the disorder,[3] researchers came to some interesting conclusions. Seventy-five percent of the cases were female, and most were in their late adolescence and early adulthood (ostensibly when insecurities are high and maturity levels low). The pain associated with the refusal or inability to see what one really is can be severe. In the study 24 percent had attempted suicide, and 72 percent suffered from personality disorders. In a sense they are afflicted by a form of "self-myopia": when they step back and look at themselves, they cannot see what is really there, and they are suffering dearly because of it.

A relevant word that has thoroughly entrenched itself into the zeitgeist of pop psychology is *denial.* As the old twelve-step joke goes, *"Denial* ain't no river in Egypt!" It's among the most common obstacles keeping people from doing what's necessary and getting the assistance they need.

Denial often works by blocking us from seeing what is apparent and/or keeping realizations at a subconscious or semiconscious level. Paradoxically, while initial denial may be advantageous in that it gives us the emotional time and space to react, like an overprotective parent, it can quickly go from protective to destructive if it hangs around too long.

My work with students who grew up in poverty and then found themselves having to compete with wealthy kids from some of the best schools in the country sheds a good deal of light on how overcoming denial can facilitate resilience, which in these cases meant remaining competitive, despite the significant head starts of their new peers.

Many of my study participants were top students in their inner-city schools only to find themselves woefully underprepared once they entered prestigious colleges. When faced with this reality, those who succeeded had to not only admit that they were now far behind but also that what they thought were decent public schools were actually often pretty crappy. This is a whole lot of humble pie for an eighteen- or nineteen-year-old to swallow, but it had to be done.

In a study myself and a colleague conducted on fifty students who exhibited resilience,[4] a full 96 percent exhibited the ability to recognize *and accept* the disadvantages they were born into and responded by seeking out necessary assistance (i.e., protective factors). Not only did they exhibit this ability, they acknowledged its essential nature. Without this prerequisite acceptance, both they and their futures would have been relegated to the usual disheartening statistics and stereotypes of low-income minority youth.

The crucial part of the dynamic is not simply the students' acknowledgment of the acute challenges that lie ahead for them, but the corequisite ability and willingness to then address those challenges through action. We will explore the connection between acceptance and action (namely *meaning*) in more detail later, but it is significant enough to warrant a brief perusal now.

Jasmine's reflection of entering a four-year college after completing her two-year associate's degree provides a glimpse into what can happen if one refuses to acknowledge and accept academic disparities and respond accordingly.

> I was so full of myself because I got a scholarship…I thought that (the scholarship) meant that, you know, I belonged, that I was ready. I remember being in my European-history class on the first day…the teacher was asking questions like what were the causes of World War I? And how did the war affect the economy? Stuff like that…I had *no* idea. I didn't even know

who fought in that war. I thought it was versus Russia. But other people knew this stuff. And it was the first day, so it's not like they just learned it in this class, they knew it already... as like background knowledge...I got really heated [angry]. I blamed the teacher, thinking that the questions were stupid. I even skipped the next class as like a protest. But stuff like that happened in my other classes, too. It was like things came easier to the other students, like they just knew stuff, almost like an inside joke. I tried to tell myself that it was no big deal, that the classes would be the same as county college [her previous school]. But I couldn't keep fooling myself. After I got my first few grades back, I knew that I was going to have to change my approach. I needed to keep a B average to keep my scholarship, and I was in trouble...Once I accepted that this was a new level, and that the same old effort and systems wouldn't work, things started to change. I committed to reading everything I could, asking lots of questions, and going for extra help at the writing lab...these are things I never had to do before, but it was a new level. And if I wanted to stay I would have to."

In Jasmine's case it becomes evident that there are several different reactions to the situation she could have had. As overwhelmed, academically insecure students often do, she could have continued to resist the reality that she had to play "academic catch up." She could have ignored or denied what she knew was happening. But in situations where bright students with mediocre or subpar educational backgrounds (like most of the students from the study) are attempting to excel in competitive and foreign environments, there is little time and room for denial, indecision or self-pity. If the students do not accept the situation and adapt swiftly and decisively, they can quickly spiral downward and easily find themselves (and their families) on the outside of the middle class looking in. These students are especially vulnerable to such spiraling because they often lack the social and financial support that wealthier students sometimes take for granted. Long story short, succumbing to denial is a luxury they simply cannot afford.

Whether it is our past addictions or a recent trauma, accepting *what is* with our eyes wide open is an important first step toward resilience. So why can it be so difficult? Let's answer that question with these questions: What if Jasmine had a huge and delicate ego? What if she viewed every setback as an attack on that ego and further evidence of her being less-than? If this were the case, it would have been unlikely that she could respond so deftly to the obstacles she faced. Like many people with delicate egos, she would have feared exposing her idealized sense of self more than she would have wanted to achieve her goals.

Accepting what is can be difficult. And in large part we can blame our friend the ego.

Beware the Distorting and Delicate Ego

The term ego has several potential meanings. We're not referring to ego as in Freud's concept of a mediating force balancing our instinctual drive and moral reasoning, but rather ego in its more common and popular usage, referring to our exaggerated senses of pride, personal value, narcissism, vanity, and self-importance. In terms of resilience, ego is like red wine—a little bit may be good for you, but too much can lead to disaster.

I recently viewed the controversial and divisive education documentary *Waiting for Superman* with a group of undergraduate prospective teachers. In presenting data on how American students stack up against other countries on academic skills assessments, the film presents the disheartening but expected answer: not very well. What was unexpected and fascinating to me was the one area where the United States did in fact *outperform every other country*—confidence. That's right. While we scored lower in math and science, our kids *feel* damn good about themselves and their academic abilities.

Evidence of increasing egos and levels of self-esteem can be found elsewhere also. In 2007 the *Los Angeles Times*[5] published an article based on the work of Jean Twenge, a San Diego State associate professor, asserting that American college students are increasingly ego-centered and narcissistic compared with previous generations. Not only does the research document this growing trend toward ego centeredness, but it also warns of the heavy price society may pay in the form of our inability to treat each other with respect and empathy.

As young America continues to convince itself that it's better and more important than it is, so grows the degree of denial as well as the refusal to acknowledge and address any of our personal flaws that may exist.

Now that I have fully transformed into a cranky *Get off of my lawn!* old man and sullied the reputation of an entire generation of young whippersnappers, let's look at specifically how and why ego (actually *managing* ego, particularly when those egos are bloated and delicate) can play such a critical role in facilitating resilience. There are two fundamental ways that ego obstructs the resilience process: *distorting meaning* and *limiting healthy risk taking*.

Recent research by Carol Dweck[6] sheds light on how this can occur and forces us to rethink some of our assumptions about the supposed benefits of building self-esteem and ego through praise. In a study that was repeated multiple times with different demographic groups, 128 students were split into two groups and given a simple IQ test. Both groups were told they excelled on the exam, but the purported reasons behind their excellence were different. One group was told they did well and that their performance was due to their being unusually *smart*. The other group was told their high scores must have been due to how exceptionally *hard they work*. In other words one group was being praised for innate intelligence (which Dweck describes as a "fixed" mind-set) and the other for the effort they exerted (a "growth" mind-set). Then all the students were asked to take another, slightly harder test. Which group do you think fared better?

Pop psychology and child-rearing clichés say, "If you *tell* a child she is intelligent, she will prove you right," thus you may think the "smart" group prevailed, but you'd be wrong. Not only did the "effort" kids do better on the second exam, but they were more eager to take it. The "intelligent" children were more reluctant and did worse. So what's going on here?

Well, in part the "intelligent" group was so invested in *protecting* their status as being smart, they were reluctant to expose themselves by putting themselves in a position of possible failure—failure that would then invalidate their views of themselves as smarter. The "effort" kids had no such compunctions because they believed it was their effort, something over which they had control, that was the difference. Therefore, the perceived risk to ego was substantially diminished. The result was eagerness to take risks and continue to put forth effort.

The "intelligent" group perceived their value as fixed and static and absolute and therefore out of their control. So in their cases they had to protect themselves through inaction. There was nothing to do or use; it just was. But the "effort" group perceived their value in what they *did*, a capacity that could grow through action. (Note that later we will spend much more time exploring the benefits of belief in the efficacy of action as compared to passivity engendered by lack of belief.)

Based on this and similar research, Dweck believes that too much praise, especially when that praise is in regard to innate qualities such as intelligence, often backfires because children become more interested in preserving their status than on taking chances and tackling new challenges. Here we see that not only does too much ego inhibit risk taking, but it also distorts the meaning of failure. If the "effort" child fails, it means he must exhibit more effort in the future. However, if the "intelligent" student fails, then all of a sudden he is no longer intelligent; it's the same antecedent with vastly different meanings.

Later we will revisit Dweck's work in terms of its implications regarding degree of belief in one's ability to affect outcomes (i.e., self-efficacy) and how valuable that can be, but for now I'd like to focus more on how too much ego, especially unchecked, can inhibit resilience.

As we have discussed, accepting reality and strategically constructing meaning are at the core of the resilience process. The problem is, a bloated and frail ego makes these crucial steps that much more difficult because it places you and your insecurities at the center of the drama. And when traumas touch a nerve in us (i.e., they threaten our ego) it is all but impossible to see and accept what is actually happening, let alone to frame it in a personally healthy and advantageous manner.

How potentially explosive and distorting can perceived attacks on the ego become? A look at the murder rates and causes provides some disturbing insights. According to a Reuters report[7] regarding the US Centers for Disease Control and Protection, personal conflicts are the most common cause of murder in the United States—more common than random violence or robberies. The report specifically sites "intimate partner violence" as a pattern that stands out. The report goes on to point out that "One third of women who were murdered were killed by a current or former spouse or partner, compared to five percent of men killed by intimate partners."

There may be multiple ways of interpreting these distressing data, but I believe that in large part these are evidence of what can happen when ego is the predominate force behind meaning, decision making, and action. All too often when it's *perceived* the ego is being threatened or challenged (e.g., when a girlfriend breaks up with a boyfriend or an ex-spouse remarries), the individual experiences what noted psychologist Daniel Goleman refers to as an "emotional hijacking," meaning the person lashes out before his or her brain has had an opportunity to "comprehend" (in other words *accept*) what is occurring and perhaps more importantly what it may or may not *mean* (refer to Goleman's salient book mentioned earlier, *Emotional Intelligence*, for a thorough review of the physiology behind an emotional hijacking). This is by no means an excuse for spousal or boyfriend or girlfriend abuse, but it is often what happens.

Notice that earlier I wrote that this can occur "when it is *perceived* that the ego is being threatened." This is the key. The trigger incident (the trauma) is not *inherently* an attack on the ego (How can it be? This thing we call "ego" is a manmade construct, a synthetic, and only exists, literally and figuratively, in our minds). It only becomes an attack due to our particular interpretation. Here we are back to separating the wheat from the chaff. Those who lead with ego lose the ability to deftly determine what traumas mean. They either greatly distort meaning or react as if they have no choice at all.

Ego's penchant for facilitating distortion—and ultimately powerlessness—is illustrated well in an ultimately comical experience relayed to me by Robert, a forty-three-year-old software engineer and father of three. After working for a large financial institution for six years, he was called into his supervisor's office one Friday afternoon and told that due to a corporate takeover and "redundancies," his position was being eliminated. Robert was so wounded and embarrassed at having been fired for the first time in his life that he immediately rushed out of his supervisor's office, avoided eye contact with his colleagues, and headed straight for the elevator.

He ended up at a bar down the street obsessing over how he was going to tell his wife and kids, and couldn't shake a feeling of intense shame and humiliation that lay at the pit of his stomach. After three beers his cell phone rang. Robert checked the caller ID and saw his boss's name. "Shit!" he thought. "What is this guy doing now, rubbing it in?" Robert thought about not answering but picked up anyway. It was indeed his boss, but to Robert's surprise he was not calling to rub it in. He called to tell Robert that he had run out so fast that he didn't have a chance to finish what he was trying to say: yes, his position was being eliminated, but they also wanted to promote him and have him run a new division of his own—this meant a 20 percent increase in salary and a vice president's title!

Robert led with his ego, and it short-circuited his ability to act reasonably and in his own best interest. Not only did he break our cardinal rule, to accept only that which is immutable and true, but his ego and emotion almost prevented him from even getting to the truth. In the end things turned out well for Robert, but think of all the times people have been tripped up by ego only to never regain their balance.

To further illustrate how ego can distort, let's take a look at a hypothetical situation where two people are facing the same challenge, but one leads with his ego while the other does not.

Both Carol and Jacob want desperately to be stockbrokers, but after many months of studying recently failed the Series 7 Examination required of anybody wishing to enter the securities industry. Their responses to this relatively significant setback illuminate the differences and consequences of "leading with ego" as compared with a more humble and rational approach.

Jacob is devastated. He views the failure as incontrovertible evidence that deep down inside he is not good enough. When people ask him how he did on the exam, he's too embarrassed to tell them. Instead he lies and says he decided to put off taking it. He refuses to retake the exam for fear of risking further failure and showing evidence of his inadequacy (just like the students in Dweck's study). His shame at having failed is so strong that he convinces himself that he is simply not cutout to be a stockbroker. He unenthusiastically decides to move on to a less lucrative and less rewarding career path—one that he won't have to take an exam, any exam, to enter.

Carol is just as disappointed by not passing but does not accept that her score is as a measure of her inherent value. She accepts her score as simply and *exclusively* a signal that she must now prepare more and better. She is grateful for having the opportunity to retake the exam and is willing to do almost anything to pass. She is open and honest with friends and colleagues about her score and seeks advice and support from them. Based on that advice and what she has learned, she designs a new study plan and approach and is scheduled to retake the exam in six months.

Unfortunately for Jacob, chiefly because of his ego, he will not be a licensed stockbroker. Not only did his ego distort what the nonpassing score "meant" but, just as important, it kept him from taking the risks necessary to live the life he really wanted. As we have seen, ego's dance partner is most often *risk aversion.* As Dweck demonstrated, when we're preoccupied with ego protection and risk avoidance, performance suffers.

A swollen and fragile ego is like a newborn baby: it yearns for protection and shelter from perceived threats—and the biggest threat to ego is potential failure. The world of entrepreneurship is a great context in which the risk aversion engendered by too much ego can be examined.

I have always been impressed by individuals who strike out on their own and start a business. Think about the temerity, the *chutzpah* it takes to say, "I can do it better, and I can do it on my own." These people often invest everything, essentially betting on themselves. Now, some might say that anyone willing to do that must have a huge ego. Maybe, but that person probably doesn't have a *fragile* ego, and he or she is definitely not *leading* with that fragile ego.

According to noted business expert and "serial entrepreneur" K. Mackillop,[9] risk aversion and protection of the ego is the greatest impediment to success in the high-stakes, high-risk, high-reward world of entrepreneurship. As Mackillop puts it, "Starting a business is not for everyone…some folks just can't cope with the thought of failure…(of) damaging one's personal brand, basically, the ego." The ego, or again the *protection* of the ego, cannot be the primary concern if you need to take risks because risk exposes the ego, and for those with delicate egos, even the *possibility* of failure is too daunting.

Resilient people are different. Most either want the reward badly enough (as we will see in the chapter on Meaning) that they are willing to expose their egos to potential threats, or (and this is probably the preferred approach) they simply do not equate failure with personal inadequacy. Once we rob failure of its ability to make us question our inherent value, then taking risks is relatively easy—there is no longer a daunting downside. This is where accepting only that which is absolutely true and eschewing the rest can play such a significant role. Yes, the thing, whatever it is, happened. But, no, is does not *necessarily* mean you are less than.

To illustrate how the mere possibility of failure can severely inhibit our ability to perform even simple tasks, think about the following scenario. I place a board one foot in the air, supported by cinderblocks on either side. The board is sturdy, two inches thick and ten inches wide, and stretches thirty feet. I place $10,000 on one end of the board and say, "If you can walk the length of the board without falling off, you may keep the $10,000." Would you do it? Of course you would. It's relatively easy. Your chances of falling off, assuming you're not drunk, are virtually nil, and even if you do fall off, you won't be hurt.

But let's say we keep everything exactly the same, but instead of one foot off the ground, the board is stretched above an elevator shaft one hundred feet in the air. Would you do it then? Probably not. But why? Everything is exactly the same. It is still highly unlikely that you will fail, but the fear of failing (and the consequence) is now so great that most of us would not even make an attempt, no matter how big the reward.

People with large and delicate egos often *artificially* raise the height of the board (the difficulty and consequences of the task) thus perceiving a board that's actually only a foot off the ground as being a hundred feet. This massively bloats the consequences of failure, thus they are afraid to even try. Ultimately, their fear of a bruised ego inhibits their taking the necessary actions to succeed.

Most resilient people are not only adept at realistically appraising the risks and rewards inherent to a task, but they are secure enough in themselves that they consistently seek out potentially rewarding challenges in the process. Assisting them along the way is a clichéd yet still healthy view of failure as teacher rather than adversary.

There are two caveats here:

- There is nothing wrong with ego per se. It is only when the ego, and its close cousin *vanity*, is excessive and/or delicate that it becomes a problem. Furthermore, let's not confuse confidence with ego. To oversimplify a complicated distinction, confidence means knowing you are good and will succeed, and ego is *having* to be good and *having* to succeed.

- Understanding on an intellectual level that a particular failure or rejection is not an indication of our value is an important first step, but simple awareness of this enlightened thinking does not automatically shield us from the sting or from our reflexive responses. The ego is not entirely rational; therefore, it does not always respond to rational arguments. Like most things, *awareness, patience,* and *reflection* can help us evolve and get where we want to be, but keep in mind they are not panaceas.

Acceptance and Liberation

One of my favorite sayings is one that many people (including my wife) think is a hollow and pointless waste of perfectly good letters and words:

"It is what it is." On one level this redundant little phrase consisting of only twelve letters says nothing, but on another it says *everything*. It serves as a critical reminder that there are some absolutes that cannot be changed. This may seem disheartening on the surface, but it can actually be quite freeing. Once something is established as immutable, we no longer have to spend precious time and energy obsessing over how we can change it. It is what it is. Permission now granted to move on.

The phrase also has a related implicit meaning that is germane to our goals here. The subtext of "It is what it is" is "and that's *all* that it is." As we've discussed, the capacity to limit acceptance to that which is absolute, and refrain from bringing along a bunch of superfluous and potentially debilitating extras in the process, is both essential and liberating.

Nathan is a former student of mine who served as a soldier in Iraq. While there, he lost his left hand as the result of an IED (improvised explosive device). I have always been both terrified and fascinated by war and combat, so when veterans are open to it, I enjoy hearing their stories. Over coffee on several occasions, I got to know Nathan and his story pretty well.

One of the things that stood out in listening to him was this unexpected relationship between acceptance and liberation. Acceptance did not come easily to him, but once it came it gave him the freedom to move his focus and energy elsewhere. Nathan put this in an e-mail to me:

> I fought it and fought it. I knew my hand was gone, but I didn't really get it or accept it...It was like it happened to someone else, not me. It was strange...Everybody told me how lucky I was to be alive, and I would say, "yeah," but the truth was I didn't feel lucky at all. I was pissed and angry but didn't really want to show it cause I had buddies from my squad who lost much more...I tried to convince myself that nothing happened, that I wasn't disfigured, that it wasn't that big a deal, but I would just get frustrated...I remember clearly

when things began to change, because it was my daughter's seventh birthday party. After the party she was sitting on my lap playing with a Barbie and she goes, "Daddy, is your hand ever going to grow back?" At first it was like getting kicked in the stomach…It was such a simple question, but I had trouble answering it. Finally, I said, "No, sweetie, it's gone."…that was a really big deal, it was like I finally could admit things were changed and I would never have my hand. It was like I could lie to myself, but with my daughter, I just couldn't…I thought it was going to be like this big thing for her, but she didn't really care…before I barely finished talking she was like, "Daddy, can we go to Disney World soon, and also can you teach me how to ride a bike?"…it made me realize that there was lots of important stuff I wanted to do and that I still could do, stuff I was looking forward to and that was important to my daughter…Not having a hand sucks, but I realized it didn't mean my life was over…I could still do all the important stuff… You know, it's like, what else can a guy ask for? The important stuff was still there. I lost my hand, that's it…Did I feel fine after that? No. But it was kind of a relief, it was like, OK we'll keep going.

Acceptance was tough for Nathan, but through reflection and his daughter's ability to help him crystallize his values, he was able to retract his initial overly assumptive interpretation of the trauma and replace it with a more limited and, I'd argue, healthy one.

Perhaps nowhere else is the inherent value and liberation of accepting reality more cherished and celebrated than in Buddhist traditions. A primary teaching of Zen Buddhism is the full and unfettered acceptance of reality. As Shunryu Suzuki wrote in her famous work *Zen Mind, Beginner's Mind*,[10] "Zen is not some fancy, special art of living. Our teaching is just to live, always in reality, in its exact sense." This concept of living in and accepting *what is* seems *so* simple and *so* straightforward, but can be *so* difficult. Committed followers of Buddhism may spend their entire lives working to increase the ease with which they accept that which *is*. Why do they do this? They've come to the conclusion that fighting reality is both exhausting and futile. They are choosing accordance rather than conflict and harmony rather than discord—instead of fighting the tides, they withdraw their oars and let the current take them.

Accepting Versus Giving In

Unfortunately, the potentially resilient among us face an apparent paradox here, one with which we will be grappling throughout this book. On one hand we are being exhorted to "go with the flow" and acquiesce to *what is*; however, we know that resilience often requires us to resist the temptation to give in to inertia, and to *actively* direct our lives. So what's a poor soul to do? I can't tell you what to do, but I can tell you what resilient people tend to do.

There is an important distinction between *accepting* and *giving in* that resilient people appear to understand intuitively. Fundamentally, while resilient people view acceptance as a starting point, others view it as an end point. Resilient people tap into the liberation associated with acceptance, using it as a springboard from which to *begin* action. For them acceptance means there are now known variables that do not require further investigation or fretting. Consequently, they can begin strategizing on how the greater goal can be achieved despite that which they can no longer influence or control. On the other hand, giving in entails getting so caught up with the overwhelming nature of what they reflexively believe the reality means—they no longer believe in their own ability to move on, so they end up not only giving in but giving up.

So, if nothing else, remember this: Acceptance ≠ Giving In

Acceptance and Judgment

Another helpful reminder when it comes to acceptance is to remember that acceptance does not *necessarily* mandate judgment. One can accept that something has occurred or that it *is* without labeling it as "good" or "bad." This is something most of us have difficulty doing. An event occurs and we immediately *know*, beyond a shadow of a doubt, that it was a good thing or a bad thing, and then we react accordingly. However, it is proven time and time again that this is a deeply flawed approach. Often an event which seemed bad initially, becomes good in retrospect—once time has passed and we can place it in a context (and vice versa). This understanding assists resilient people by preventing their overreacting and/or wasting of time and emotional energy.

This idea of reducing our reflexive tendency to immediately judge an event is also in line with Zen Buddhist teachings. Zen Buddhism implores us to accept what is and to practice resisting our desire to respond emotionally and with conviction each and every time something even semi-significant happens.

Barbara and the Stolen Car

The details of the following parable are original, but essentially it is an updated version of a well-known Zen story about a famer who finds a horse. One of the purposes is to illustrate why spending lots of time and energy judging certain events can be a waste of time and emotional energy. As a point of information, let's begin with the premise that the protagonist, Barbara, is highly evolved and has bought wholeheartedly into the above thinking.

Barbara leaves her office late one evening with her coworker, Lyn, only to find that her car has been stolen. "Oh, Barbara, this is so terrible," Lyn says. Barbara looks at the space where her car was and simply responds,

"Maybe." A few days later, Barbara tells Lyn that the insurance company will buy her a brand-new car to replace the old one that was stolen. Lyn responds, "Wow! That is great. Aren't you lucky! Having your car stolen was actually a *good* thing!" And again, Barbara says, "Maybe."

A week later Barbara drives home in her brand-new car, but unfamiliar with its acceleration and handling, she crashes into a highway divider. Though not seriously hurt, the emergency medical technician (EMT), who Barbara can't help but notice is both cute and apparently kind, insists that she get checked out at the local hospital. Lyn meets her there and says, "Oh my, it is so terrible that you were in that accident! Too bad your other car was stolen." Barbara responds, "Maybe."

Several days later the EMT, Larry, calls Barbara and asks her out on a date. The two have a wonderful time and decide to see each other again. And while Barbara does like him, she senses something disconcerting about his demeanor that she can't quite put her finger on. Upon hearing the two had a good first date, Lyn says, "You are so lucky to find a cute guy who is also nice. Larry seems great! Maybe your car getting stolen was actually a *good* thing." And, as predicted, Barbara responds with "Maybe."

Cue soap opera narrator's deep voice: "Will Barbara and Larry live happily ever after? Is Larry what he seems to be? Was the car getting stolen a "good" or "bad" thing? Will Lyn get her *own* life?"

Who knows? All of the people and events in the story are fluid, interdependent, and incomplete. And unlike Lyn, Barbara appears to know this and thus does not get too up or down as the events unfold. Barbara's attitude makes accepting reality a bit easier. Because she does not constantly label events as good or bad, she can better take them as they come.

Remembering Barbara's story can be helpful when we find ourselves reflexively labeling and judging the inevitable peaks and valleys of life.

We can *try* at least to and accept that it indeed has happened without automatically infusing the occurrence with a positive or negative meaning.

As with much of what we have been discussing in regards to becoming resilient, this is not easy. To a large extent, we are hardwired to judge events as good or bad, or threatening or comforting, so that we can respond appropriately and rapidly. But in relatively minor situations where labeling the incident serves no direct purpose, accepting with a wait-and-see attitude often makes the most sense.

Making It Work for You

TIS / TIS Not

My wife is a vegan, which, to loosely quote Jules from the film *Pulp Fiction*, "pretty much makes me one, too." When shopping for shoes, bags and coats, she tries to avoid buying any products made from animals. What constantly surprises us is how organic, natural, and real many of the synthetic leather products now look and feel. In the past it seemed obvious what was animal and what was man-made (what we used to call "pleather"). Now we often have to check and double check labels. This almost imperceptible difference between natural (what is) and synthetic (what we fabricate) parallels the struggle of acceptance. The fact that we can be easily confused about what is real and what we fabricate is why taking a slower and more deliberate approach to acceptance is so often necessary.

Using the TIS / TIS Not T-Chart

The T-Chart located at the end of this chapter can be used as a helpful graphic organizer to differentiate between that which is *absolute* and that which, to use a legal term, is simply hearsay.

1. In the "Event/Trauma" section, succinctly with as few words as possible, identify the event or trauma that is at issue.

2. On a separate piece of paper list all of the *negative stuff* that comes to mind when you think about the *consequences* of the event/trauma and what it might mean to you. Do not worry about categorizing or judging their validity. If they come to mind and bother you, list them.

3. Review what you've written, then under the TIS section of the chart list only the absolute truths from your list of negative stuff. These are truths/consequences that cannot, no matter what, be disputed. Do this as dispassionately as possible. Remember, these are *only items with which no sane person could argue*. It very well may be only one item. Very often it will look almost the same as what you put in your initial *Event/Trauma* description at the top.

4. Under the TIS Not section write down all the other items you listed. These may be *possible* interpretations/meanings or even *probable ones*, but they are *not* absolute. These may include fears, worst-case scenarios, things that *may* happen, and/or even things that are *likely* to happen.

5. Now take a thick, permanent, black marker (if you have one handy) and draw a large X through the right column. *These things do not really exist outside of your mind.* They may come to fruition, or they may not. But right now they are only projections.

OK, now review the columns (if you are like most people, your right column will be considerably longer than your left).

Now, we have good news, better news, and bad news (if you are like most people, you'll want the bad news first). The bad news is that the baseline trauma is still there, and you can never erase its presence. The good news is that you now have permission to stop trying. Yes, you must accept, but you must only accept the stuff on the left. The better news is that all the dreaded stuff in the right column has been manufactured, either by you or society—or both. And as with anything that has been created, it can also be destroyed. It is possible those things may come to fruition, but it is not an inevitable eventuality—it is not destined. Once you accept the left, you can then go to work on the right.

The *sample* TIS /TIS Not T-Chart provided may help illustrate better how we can use this tool to promote healthy acceptance.

For the sample we will use a fictional woman named Nancy. She is a forty-year-old mother of two daughters, eleven and thirteen. Her ex-husband, Randy, the primary breadwinner in the family, recently shocked Nancy by springing a divorce on her and then running off to Venezuela with their housekeeper. Nancy was completely unaware of the relationship and had not suspected her husband of any infidelity. Not only is she stunned, but she feels like an idiot for not noticing what was going on.

In reviewing the sample, notice how brief and to the point both the *Event/Trauma* and TIS sections are. In fact they are virtually the same thing. But that is not what is really bothering Nancy. It is the litany of worries to the right, many of which are tied directly to her ego.

Even though Nancy is fictitious, and thus we do not have any concrete background on her, using extrapolation and inference, let's review each item on the TIS Not side. What we will see is that ultimately they are possibilities, some more possible than others, but they are far from inevitable and absolute truths.

1.*"I was a bad wife."*

Nancy may or may not have been a "bad wife," but most rational people would not infer that the spouse who *didn't* unexpectedly run off with the maid would have been the "bad" spouse. Most would infer this to be a complete fabrication induced by low self-esteem and/or perceptions of societal ideals.

2. *"My parents are going to blame me."*

We don't know Nancy's parents, but unless they are mean-spirited and vindictive people, they probably would not blame her. If they did blame her, however, most objective outsiders would find their actions reprehensible. If Nancy discussed these issues with these objective folks (and or a good therapist), it is likely she would eventually come to this same conclusion.

3. *"I am a failure."*

Like item one above, most rationale people would not come to this conclusion. Nancy is correlating a failed marriage, regardless of the reasons behind the failure, with *personal* failure. She may hold onto this conclusion, but if she discussed the feeling with people who loved and/ or cared about her deeply, it is likely she would reject this idea.

4. *"No man will ever want me again."*

This is highly unlikely. Maybe in 1950 it would have been difficult to secure another mate, but not now. There may be some men who prefer not dating divorced women, but the majority would be open to it. Ego and fear are clouding Nancy's judgment. It is likely that eventually this idea will be proven false.

5. *"My kids will be psychologically damaged."*

Nancy's children will probably suffer emotionally from the sudden divorce, but it probably won't lead to "psychological damage." Most psychologists would tell Nancy that a divorce alone is rarely enough to considerably derail a child's psychosocial development. In fact if her children see Nancy express the qualities necessary to bounce back from this unexpected blow, they could benefit a great deal from having such a positive and resilient role model for a parent. Finally, given that about half of all marriages now end in divorce, Nancy's children will hardly be alone (In fact it may even help them fit it!). While Nancy's initial fear regarding how the divorce will affect her children may be common, it is miles from a fait accompli.

6. *"I won't be able to afford to stay in the house and will have to move."*

7. *"We will have to go on food stamps."*

The financial challenges that Nancy now faces are real and pressing; however, these particular results, moving and food stamps, may or may not come to fruition. There are a myriad variables, possibilities, and possible financial resources that will have to be explored before any of these outcomes will be determined. This is one of those areas that she simply does not have enough data to come to a conclusion on. Nancy will probably have to make some changes to her financial life, but nobody, including her, knows all that will need to be done and what the consequences may be. Perhaps she will be forced to go back to school and end up getting a better job than her husband had—who knows? It is too early for such definitive statements. Also, her response to item seven regarding food stamps appears to be another instance of an overly active ego. Most compunctions about food stamps stem from shame and fear of embarrassment.

All of the stuff on Nancy's right side are possibilities, fears, and potential consequences, but none are absolute foregone conclusions, and they need not be accepted, at least at that moment. So in effect we have greatly reduced the causes of Nancy's anxiety.

I understand it's unrealistic to expect people caught in the middle of such traumas to completely divorce themselves (no pun intended) from anxiety-inducing projections of fear and panic. However, if we can reduce the number and/or intensity of these projections, even just a little, isn't it worth it?

Hopefully you now grasp the potential value of our first variable, *acceptance*. We can now move on to its close (and more fun, I promise) cousin, *meaning*.

TIS /TIS Not T-Chart (Sample)

Event/Trauma: Randy and I are now divorced.

TIS (It is)	TIS Not (It is Not)
Reality (That which is <u>indisputable</u>/<u>incontrovertible</u> and <u>absolute</u>)	**Interpretation** (That which is <u>debatable,</u> <u>disputable,</u> and <u>ultimately</u> <u>fabricated</u>)
• I am now a divorced woman. • Randy is now gone.	• I was a bad wife. • My parents are going to blame me. • I am a failure. • No man will ever want me again. • My kids will be psychologically damaged. • I won't be able to afford to stay in the house and will have to move. • We will have to go on food stamps.

TIS /TIS Not T-Chart

Event/Trauma: _____

TIS (It is)	TIS Not (It is Not)
Reality (That which is <u>indisputable</u>/ <u>incontrovertible</u> and <u>absolute</u>)	**Interpretation** (That which is <u>debatable</u>, <u>disputable</u>, and <u>ultimately</u> <u>fabricated</u>)

CHAPTER 3:
MEANING

"I always wanted a convertible!"

"So what do you want to be when you grow up?"

We have all been asked this seemingly innocuous, even encouraging, question at various times in our lives. Usually we get this question as children or adolescents, and it gives us a chance to fantasize, even if at the time we don't see it as such. But unfortunately (or fortunately if you believe in that ubiquitous bumper sticker adage, "Not All Who Wander Are Lost") some of us must grapple with this unsettling question as adults.

It's an important question, and when people ask it, it usually demonstrates their sincere interest and concern for you and your well-being. However, (surprise, surprise) I would like to suggest an improvement to the question, a suggestion informed by our desire to promote resilience. Instead of "What do you want to be when you grow up?" we should ask, "What do you *need* to be when you grow up?"

If you really want to support someone's ultimate and enduring well-being, this is the question to ask. If you do go ahead and pose this question to a friend or loved one, don't settle for a quick or hasty answer. In order for the response to really be worthwhile, most people will have some soul-searching to do first. To answer this question well, we must dig deep into ourselves, past what we've been *told* was valuable, past what seems practical, past our egos, past social convention, past our insecurities—deep within, behind the cobwebs of your inner self. We must get to that place that is uniquely ours, where our deepest passions and desires reside. If we can discover what it is we really *need* to be and do, our journey toward resilience will not only be more manageable but ultimately more rewarding as well. Spending time in that place on a regular basis is a key to resilience.

Like learning to ride a bicycle or drive a car, you can get guidance and help with this endeavor, but ultimately the search for what is meaningful must be conducted alone. As Viktor Frankl wrote in his classic *Man's Search for Meaning,*[1] "Man's search for meaning is the primary motivation in his life…This meaning is unique and specific in that it must and can be fulfilled by him alone; only then does it achieve a significance which will satisfy his own *will* to meaning."

In order for this sense of meaning to engender the gravitas necessary to facilitate our endurance during the often stressful resilience journey, it must be unearthed in personal and private moments of intense honesty and clarity. If this sense of meaning is indeed anchored to some core part of who we *are* or *have* to be, it can then be an incredibly powerful tool. As Friedrich Nietzsche famously said, "He who has a *Why* to live for can bear almost any *How*." Consequently, we will focus on ways to cultivate our personal *whys*, as well as how the *whys* serve as high-octane fuel for our resilience-building machinery.

Returning to our formula, R = A + M + Ac, acceptance means acquiescing to the stripped-down essential truth of whatever trauma or issue we face, basically swallowing what may be a very bitter, little pill. Tempted as we may be to try and dress it up, this process is rarely, if ever, any fun at all.

The M (Meaning) step on the other hand can be barrel-of-monkeys fun, at least in comparison to the first one. Now *we* get to *choose*, within reason, both how we will interpret the remaining effects of the trauma and its implications as well as how we can utilize that which is personally valuable to us to maximize the potency of our chosen interpretations. In short while acceptance is about objective truth, meaning is about subjective reality.

Figure three below represents the two distinct yet related modes of meaning we will be discussing throughout this chapter. The first involves constructing *interpretations* of the trauma that are *personally beneficial* yet still firmly rooted in reality (i.e., *legitimate*). The second relates to uncovering and affirming levels of *meaningfulness,* in other words the degree to which we *legitimately* (i.e., truly/actually) believe in the *personal value* of our recovery.

Two Modes of Meaning

Issue/Trauma/Event

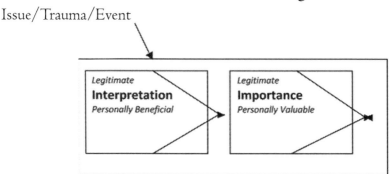

Figure 3

You'll notice that both modes contain the word "legitimate." The individual must earnestly and deeply believe in the *legitimacy*, the *authenticity* of both their interpretations of the trauma, *and* the importance/value of their chosen path to recovery. As we'll see, if the individual feels even the least bit insincere or unsure about her interpretations or lacks a deep and heartfelt belief in the value of her ultimate recovery, then she will not have the requisite energy reserves to do what is necessary in the action step in order to realize that recovery. Finally, the arrows in the box are indicators that if done well, both phases work to propel us forward by putting us in an optimal frame of mind to then take full advantage of the action step.

Crafting Meaning

In order to begin learning to craft meaning (i.e., our interpretation mode), we'll start by taking out our figurative red pens and editing the popular saying, "Everything happens for a reason." We're going to change this moderately helpful adage to the significantly more empowering, "Things happen, and we can then *provide* a reason." The former version implies that reasons for phenomena are preordained and absolute (thus immutable), while the latter acknowledges the often arbitrary nature of the world and encourages us to actively and strategically invest meaning *after* the fact.

There are two specific advantages to ascribing (or identifying) reasons and purposes (meanings) for our experiences. The first is that once there is a reason, the event can be *almost* magically transformed from obstacle to tool. Let's say I get fired from my job. If I don't ascribe a personally significant reason for the firing, then all I am left with is anger and resentment (and way too much free time on my hands). In this scenario there is no springboard, no push, no opportunity revealed. I'm just pissed off. The firing is simply an obstacle to my moving on and seeking fulfillment.

On the other hand, if I couch the firing as providence, as a message from the universe telling me that I'd be better off spending my forty hours a week doing something else—now we're in business, now we're "cookin' with gas" as the old-timers might say. The event—the firing—has been transformed into an instrument for growth and development. The event occurred and *I* provided the meaning.

Now some of the more cynical among you may be thinking this seems contrived, that we're kidding ourselves when we look for opportunity in an inherently "bad" event. To you I'd say, you may be right, but in case you haven't heard, being right is often the booby prize in life, a pyrrhic victory that can leave us feeling righteous but psychosocially destitute.

Yes this process can be a bit contrived, but we should be grateful for it. It *is* often artificial to paint the negative and the hurtful with the bright pinks, lime greens, and periwinkle blues of potential and possibility. But so what? As long as your interpretations are legitimate on some level, they can then be useful. Furthermore, *it is precisely because it is unnatural and fabricated that it can be so valuable.* This unnatural process really means empowerment—it means choice—it moves us *closer* to creating our reality and away from victimhood.

Now, this does not mean that an event can't suck also, it can. An event or occurrence can be 99 percent horrible, but that does not negate the 1 percent that's potentially not. If you can manage to identify and use that 1 percent to your personal advantage, you are not being disingenuous. You are honestly assessing and managing the situation. Thus, when faced with apparently harmful events, ideally we should all become silver lining factories. We should churn out as many *legitimately* positive or potentially beneficial outcomes as we possibly can. This is not easy, precisely because it is so unnatural. Our natural tendencies are often to close our eyes, curl up in a fetal position sucking our thumbs, and hope things get better. But as I said, unlike with food and beauty, natural is not always better.

The second primary advantage to ascribing meaning is that it facilitates our learning from the event. If I believe that there is no personally relevant reason for my being fired, then I will not ask what can be learned. There is nothing to learn because it just happened, like a leaf falling from a tree in November, or a dog chasing a car. But if I see purpose in, or benefit from, the event, then I can come right out and ask—what can I learn from this experience? Maybe I'll learn that the job really wasn't for me or that you can't trust your boss or that three-hour lunch breaks are not such a good idea, whatever. When we learn something from an event, we're actually infusing it with meaning, and the meaning is the particular lesson learned.

What about the Really Bad Stuff?

There are some events that are so unspeakably ghastly, that even the most skilled worker in the silver lining factory may suffer from silver lining maker's block and be at a loss. When a child is killed, there is a sexual assault, or a person becomes paralyzed, what then? What can we possibly reap from such horror? A lot, and often more than one could from the more pedestrian traumas people face. In fact I'd venture that generally speaking the depth and profundity of the lessons we learn and the knowledge we gain (as well as the impact we can then have on others) are commensurate with the severity of the traumas we endure.

Think about which events in your own life inspired the most growth, the most altruism, the most empathy in you. I'd bet you dollars to donuts those events were among the most painful and traumatic as well. Thus, learning from our great traumas does not mean we will be pain free or that we will be glad they occurred, but once they have occurred and we've paid the price, we may as well reap some of the rewards.

In a popular TED (Technology, Entertainment, Design) presentation, Stacey Kramer describes a precious gift that she had received five months earlier, a gift that has done amazing things for her. According to her, it has

- Brought her family together,
- Reconnected her with old friends,
- Redefined her sense of spirituality and faith,
- Expanded her vocabulary,
- Helped her meet new people, and
- Provided her with an eight-week vacation as well as access to a lifetime of "good drugs."

She then reveals that this gift was a golf-ball-sized brain tumor.

In all honesty I felt uncomfortable watching and listening to her. Referring to a brain tumor as a gift did not sit well with me. And while she does go on to say that she would not wish this gift on others, she also says that she "wouldn't change her experience," for all of the reasons listed above. So is Stacey Kramer crazy? Is she a liar? Is she still suffering the effects of her illness? I don't know. But if you asked me if she's resilient, the answer would be a resounding yes.

However she managed to do it, she has crafted multiple and profoundly rewarding meanings from her illness. And by sharing her story with the world, she is providing levels of insight, wisdom, empathy, and inspiration that she simply couldn't have had she not experienced what she did.

The concept of "paying the price" is a key. While the negatives are real, and we've endured them, there is no rule that says we must continue paying for them in perpetuity. Resilient people limit the amount of time they allow themselves to be punished by traumas, even if they may have contributed in some way to the trauma itself.

In the wildly and widely popular *The Four Agreements*,[2] Dr. Don Miguel Ruiz gets at the aberrant, almost perverted, human tendency of doing this when he writes, "How many times do we pay for one mistake? The answer is a thousand times. The human is the only animal on Earth that pays a thousand times for the same mistake. The rest of the animals pay once for every mistake they make. But not us."

Emotional self-chastisement is not a switch that can easily be turned off, but we would all do well to be reminded that it is not an eternal requirement either.

The Art of Reframing

According to noted resilience researcher Dr. Steven J. Wolin,[3] one of the ways that potentially resilient individuals harvest meaning from trauma is by reflecting on the incident and identifying ways to *change how they perceive* themselves in relation to it. Wolin refers to this process as "reframing." And while Wolin's focus is specifically on how individuals who suffered traumas as children could use this approach to better cope as adults, I've observed resilient adults effectively using this technique in a variety of contexts, and have identified several ways that it can be practiced and fostered.

Let's say you had an employee whom you supervised but, due to budget cuts, had to let go. You then find out that at about the same time you fired him, his wife left him for another man. Several days later you show up for work on a Monday morning and hear from a coworker that this former employee took his own life over the weekend, leaving no note.

So why did he kill himself? Was it because you fired him? Was it because his wife left him? Was it a combination of these events? Or was it something completely different? The fact is you don't know and probably never will. You may become racked with guilt, assuming he committed suicide because you fired him. You may begin contemplating ways you could have handled it better—maybe there were some other budget cuts you could have made instead, or perhaps you could have made him part-time instead of fully firing him. But it's just as likely the firing was *not* the cause. Therefore, assuming it reduces your guilty conscience, why not reframe the cause of the suicide with the wife's leaving as the primary cause? This theory is just as plausible and has the added benefit of providing a degree of emotional reprieve for you.

One of the most ubiquitous emotional crises people face at one time or another is being dumped by a boyfriend or girlfriend they really liked. How common are these figurative attacks on the heart? There are literally thousands, if not millions, of songs devoted to this phenomenon, not to mention all the "boy meets girl—boy loses girl" movies, books, plays, and television programs. Note that the primary culprit of the emotional pangs is usually the conclusion that the breakup occurred because there was something inherently wrong with or broken about us. Reflecting on your own breakups, I bet you'll find this to be true. This supposition (valid or not) can severely wound our self-esteem and leave us feeling worthless and unwanted.

Now that I have depressed you by triggering memories of your all-time worst breakups, let's get to the reframing strategy. One of the ways we can mitigate the severity of the emotional wallop is by identifying a viable alternative for *why* they broke up with us. In other words we can ask this question: aside from my not being good enough, what are some other *plausible* reasons why he or she broke up with me? The potential power of coming up with an alternative that is reasonable can be startling.

The Magic Kiss

An experience a friend of mine had really drives this point home. A few years out of college he began dating a lovely young woman whom he met while jogging in Manhattan's Central Park. The morning after their first date, he called me with an uncharacteristically animated affect and informed me that he had just met the woman he would marry. As you might have guessed, given the premise and purpose of my telling this story, this is not what happened. After dating for several months, not only did she break up with him, but she broke a long-standing social courtesy by doing it over the phone! She provided very vague reasons for her desire to end it, something about "growing apart" and "wanting different things," but there must have been something wrong with his phone because all he could hear was, "You're a worthless loser and not good enough."

He wallowed for the next several months, rarely leaving his apartment. When we *were* able to drag him out to a bar or restaurant, he would periodically leave the table and call her, even though she had stopped taking his calls almost immediately after the breakup—"Damn caller ID!" he used to say. Eventually she even changed her number.

After a while he slipped into a mild depression, and then he stopped returning *my* calls. I figured, like most people, he just needed some time, so I left him alone.

Less than a month went by when *he* called *me* sounding surprisingly chipper. "You sound good," I said. "What's going on?" I assumed one of two things: either they had gotten back together or he had met somebody else. But to my surprise neither of these was the case. What did happen was both more unexpected and more telling.

Apparently, while still pining away for her, he began to wait outside of her apartment (exactly *why*, I'm not sure, but the word *stalker* did come to my mind). Then one morning, from across the street, he sees her walk out of her building holding hands with a figure he could not fully make out. He then saw the two kiss and almost passed out with jealously. In telling me the story, he said his heart sank and he began to lose his breath. But as the distant couple got closer to him, he saw that the person holding her hand was another woman.

It took a few moments for the shock to recede, but almost immediately and just like *that* (cue snapping fingers), his depression lifted, and he began to feel better. His breathing returned to normal, and he felt a sense of levity overtake him. His feelings of not being good enough quickly dissipated, and he felt somehow refreshed. In an instant he reframed the reason for the breakup. It changed from him being wholly inadequate to simply her being a lesbian. And this, as he interpreted it, had nothing to do with him or his value as a man. And with that he felt restored.

Ultimately, there is much we and my friend will never know for certain. Did she really break up with him because she was having feelings for another woman, or was he really not good enough? Or was it something completely different? In this case it really doesn't matter. Once my friend decided that it was indeed because of her latent lesbianism, which to him was the plausible if not likely explanation, he felt significantly better.

Meaning and Struggle

We will begin our exploration of the second mode of meaning, *importance*, by looking at its close relationships with struggle and endurance.

Identifying and cultivating meaning in and around our traumas can not only help us see their fleeting temporal nature but can also help us transcend their suffocating grasp. When we really believe there is meaning *inherent* to the struggle, we are in a better position to endure and overcome. Going back to Frankl gives us the chance to delve into these concepts more deeply. After the initial publication of his book, he proposed the following formula correlating the variables *despair, suffering,* and *meaning.*

Despair = Suffering − Meaning

(I bet you didn't think we'd be doing this much math!)

Essentially, Frankl is saying *despair* emerges only when and if the *meaning* associated with our suffering is inadequate. Suffering may be necessary, but we need not *despair* if we have ample meaning.

Too abstract and philosophical? Let's concretize things a bit with a fictitious scenario. There is a man and his pregnant wife snorkeling off the coast of Malaysia. The two get separated by the powerful current, and he ends up splitting his head on a rock. The next thing he knows he washes up on a deserted island. But unlike in the movies and on TV, the island is not a government experiment gone bad nor the lair of an evil genius, and he won't run into Gilligan. It's just a small desolate patch of sand and a few scattered coconut trees.

The man is there for several months and *suffering* each and every day. He is hungry, thirsty, and scared. He sleeps on a bed made of leaves and twine, using a coconut wrapped in his tattered shirt for a pillow. He wakes frequently throughout the night hoping that his situation is only a dream but quickly realizes that he really is stranded and alone. Despair is about to overtake him like aggressive storm clouds, and once it does it's only a matter of time before he gives up and dies.

But if the man can view each moment he stays alive as an incremental step closer to eventually reuniting with his wife and meeting his unborn child, his level of despair can be kept to a minimum. He will endure the suffering with a sense of purpose, which will keep despair at bay. He will use this intense meaning as fuel to endure and do what is necessary to stay alive. Each action he takes, from building a hut to gathering firewood to spearing fish with a sharpened stick, is a figurative step toward his family. By infusing his suffering with meaning, he is more willing and able to endure that suffering and do what needs doing. As long has he continues in this vein, despair will not make camp in his mind, and the possibility of uniting with his family will remain.

Will he get off the island? Maybe—maybe not. But again, that's not really the point. What is the point is that his likelihood of survival increases as he continues to focus on what really matters to him.

Figure four below is a simple yet powerful reminder of the direct connections between *meaning* and *endurance* levels. Essentially, the more personally meaningful something is, the more one is willing/able to endure in order to achieve or protect it. These two variables are continually feeding one another and together set the stage for resilience.

Going back to our friend Nietzsche, if our meaning level (the why) is powerful, our willingness to endure (the what) rises. If we find the situation moderately important, then our endurance level will follow. And, like seeing a penny on the street as we are walking by, if the importance level is low, we will barely break stride in order to address it.

Ironically, it is not only that meaning levels determine endurance levels, but endurance levels can actually work to reinforce meaning. The sweat and sacrifice we invest in service of what we believe is meaningful actually reinforces that meaning. It is as if our mind says, *Wow! You must really want this. Look at all you are willing to do and put up with!* This is represented by the cyclical arrows connecting the two variables.

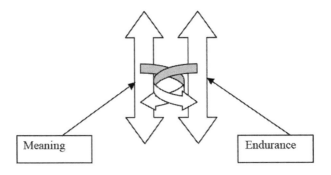

Figure 4 Meaning and Endurance

Lucky for us we don't have to be herded into a concentration camp nor stranded on a deserted island to identify and utilize meaning. We see examples of people doing this every day. Why do you think aspiring actors work ten-hour shifts as waiters and waitresses? Because they enjoy disgruntled diners, constant complaining, and plastering perpetual smiles on their faces? They do it because they want to be an actor *so* badly that they are willing to endure almost anything to sustain that possibility, regardless of how remote it might be. Now, you or I may be unwilling to put up with those headaches just for a long shot at making it as an actor, but all that means is that it's not that important to us. If deep down inside we *need* to do something, if it is *that* important to us, then there is no telling what we'd endure.

Before we get deep into strategies of creating and using meaning to promote resilience, let's look at some of the ample evidence for why and how meaning and purpose can be so beneficial.

Eudaemonic Versus Hedonistic Well-Being

The term "eudaemonic well-being" refers to the positive state that comes from being engaged in personally meaningful activities. The powerful feelings of significance and personal value that come from engaging in activities like caring for a loved one, creating art, or overcoming a fear, can provide people with *sustained* feelings of contentedness and fulfillment. Our understanding of the value and uniqueness of this state can be enhanced by contrasting it to what researchers sometimes refer to as "hedonistic" well-being, which tends to be more ephemeral and less substantive.

Hedonistic well-being is usually defined as the presence of good feelings and absence of negative ones—for example, getting that raise you wanted, winning money in Atlantic City, or buying a new luxury car. And while these are apparently "good" things, the positive feelings rarely last. The writer Augusten Burroughs[4] succinctly captured the fleeting nature of hedonistic joy when he compared it to "a long sneeze." Sneezing feels great, but it doesn't leave much of a legacy. In fact what you are left with is not very pleasant at all. Once it's done it's done, as if it never even happened. Actually, as we will soon see, persistent pursuit of hedonistic goals, especially at the exclusion of more eudaemonic ones, can contribute to multiple negative effects on both our physical and mental health.

The integral role of meaning in the process of living a "good life" goes as far back as Aristotle. The Greek philosopher coined the term "eudaemonia" (derived from the Greek words *eu,* meaning good, and *daimon,* meaning a deity), which loosely translates as human wellness and flourishing. Aristotle was not a big fan of immediate or hedonistic pleasures and warned that pursuit of such fleeting interests would distract people from more meaningful and ultimately more healthful endeavors. Thousands of years later, research is proving him prophetic.

In 2010 researchers from San Diego State University[5] wanted to better understand trends of psychopathologies (e.g., rates of depression, paranoia, etc.) over multiple generations. These researchers did not just look at a few people here and there: they analyzed the records of over sixty-three thousand college students and thirteen thousand high school students from 1938 to 2007. What they found was as startling as it was disturbing. They concluded that more recent generations are *five times more likely to suffer from psychopathologies*. No, that is not a typo—five times. While this is highly disconcerting on its own, more relevant to our exploration of meaning is their hypothesis as to *why* this is the case. The researchers write, "The results best fit a model citing cultural shifts toward extrinsic goals, such as materialism and status and away from intrinsic goals, such as community, meaning in life, and affiliation." In other words this dramatic and frightening increase in psychosocial suffering may be due in large part to the trend of people moving away from eudaemonic pursuits in favor of more hedonistic ones.

Particularly relevant to our focus on using eudaemonic endeavors to encourage our expending the necessary effort to complete a task is research by Alan Waterman[6] concluding, among other things, that we will actually *enjoy* exerting effort if we are engaged in what he terms "personally salient activities"— that is, activities which hold particular *meaning to us*.

Let's stop and meditate on how crucial this concept is to facilitating our resilience. For what is the process of resilience if not maintaining the energy and fortitude necessary to *do* what is necessary to survive and thrive, even when it is particularly difficult to do so? Not only does a deep sense of meaning empower us to do this, but it can actually make the actions somewhat enjoyable.

To gain a more comprehensive understanding of how we benefit from engaging in eudaemonic approaches to wellness, we can look to the work of psychologists Richard Ryan an Edward Deci.[7] They emphasize that a primary difference between eudaemonic and hedonic approaches to wellness is that while hedonistic pursuits emphasize *outcomes*, eudaemonic ones focus on *process*. This difference is essential to our discussion on resilience, for resilience at its essence is a *process* rather than an outcome. There will always be new challenges and setbacks, so a disproportionate emphasis on outcomes leaves one vulnerable to a roller coaster ride of radically uneven emotions. This is why we speak of increasing your resilience *capacity,* (i.e., the thickness of your rubber). In general resilience is not about overcoming that one big hurdle and then having an eternal celebration. It's about continued readiness and practice. Eudaemonic approaches to wellness can provide us the tools we need to effectively engage in the ongoing nature of resilience.

One of the counterintuitive aspects of placing value on *process*-based eudaemonic activities over *outcomes*-based hedonistic ones is that in many contexts, striving and hustling to achieve something feeds our sense of well-being *more* than sitting back and relaxing once a goal has been met.

In *Rush: Why You Need and Love the Rat Race,*[8] former White House Director of Economic Policy Todd G. Buchholz makes this very claim. Buchholz convincingly argues that we *need* the rush that comes from competition and striving, and that we thrive when in their active service. Following this line of thinking, Buchholz concludes that we should view retirement as an *enemy* to be avoided at all costs. He even goes as far as to say that if we don't it will eventually "make us stupid."

While I would encourage you to take Mr. Buchholz's arguments with a grain of salt, and to think about your particular personality before heeding his advice, I do think he makes some valid points. The most important one being that very often when we are focused and engaged in what really matters to us, when we are in a state of "flow," we are most fulfilled and energized.

Michael Steger is a Colorado State University psychology professor[9] and directs the Laboratory for the Study of Meaning and Quality of Life there. Steger has devoted much of his professional life to studying how people create meaning in their lives and the potential benefits of the process. He believes that among those searching for meaning in life, there are two types, which we can call "lookers" and "finders." *Lookers* are those who go on endless and evolving journeys searching for meaning; whereas *finders* find what is meaningful to them relatively quickly, believe in it wholeheartedly, and stop there. Perhaps not surprisingly, the group that is quick to see meaning, and sticks with that sense of meaning (i.e., the *finders*), tends to be happier. Contradicting much of what I've written, in this case, at least, it seems that it's not about the journey but rather the destination.

Steger's findings correspond with statistics that will be explored later indicating that religious believers, as opposed to nonbelievers, tend to live less stressful lives and enjoy a variety of mental and physical health advantages. Many people find the straightforward and direct provision of meaning engendered by religious doctrine to be significant, and experience invaluable benefits of formal membership in religious organizations. Once these folks buy into the meaning provided to them by their religious affiliation, they can spend less time wondering about the meaning of their lives and more time simply living.

Unfortunately, this does not mean those among us who are still searching for definitive meaning can simply *choose* a path that seems good and will ourselves to believe. It doesn't work that way. That's called delusion. If we don't deeply and earnestly believe in the authenticity of the doctrine, it is unlikely we will reap the benefits. In other words the sincerity (or lack thereof) behind our actions mediates the potential payoff.

This is similar to the well-documented pleasure people experience when engaging in altruistic endeavors. The efforts must be sincere and heartfelt in order to achieve the desired effect. According to research done by Dr. Netta Weinstein from of the University of Essex in England and Dr. Richard Ryan from the University of Rochester,[10] if one feels even moderately coerced or pressured into doing good deeds, the personal benefits are unlikely to be achieved. Ultimately, the bottom line is that *voluntary* actions based on authentic personal meanings and truths are prerequisites to reaping the benefits of munificence as well-meaning.

One of the common ways people create meaning in their lives, and enjoy the benefits we've been discussing, is by doing for others. Germane to our focus on resilience, many go down this path in direct response to their personal tragedies. A large number of charities and foundations devoted to specific illnesses and conditions owe their existence and continued survival to those who suffered either directly or indirectly from a particular affliction, and then infused their suffering with meaning by creating said charity. The actor Christopher Reeve was one of those people.

On May 27, 1995, Christopher D'Olier Reeve was paralyzed from a spinal cord injury resulting from an equestrian accident. In response he and his wife joined up with an existing charity, the American Paralysis Association, and eventually gave their names and high profile to the group. Seventeen years later, the Christopher & Dana Reeve Foundation has funded over eighty million dollars in research aimed at curing spinal cord injury.

Think about how much would not have been done, how many people would not have been helped, had Reeve not committed himself to using his trauma to help others. Just after the accident, Reeve was quoted as saying, "I have always been a crusader for causes I believe in. This time the cause found me."

As we've discussed, the unique power of personal meaning often encourages us to put up with things on the way to our goals that others would not. In their extensive research on meaning and work, economists Stuart Bundereson and Jeffery Thompson[11] found direct correlations between willingness to sacrifice and degree of meaning. In particular they looked at the backbreaking and relatively low paying occupation of zookeeper. Many zoo workers view working closely with animals as the ultimate way to spend one's time and contentedly engage in the animals' daily lives without complaint. Yes, they have to get up at dawn. Yes, they have to work weekends. And, yes, they have to clean feces out of the cages. But they are passionate about animals and view these seemingly unpleasant tasks as small prices to pay in order to do what they love. As the authors of the study point out, there is a word for when people simply *must* engage in a certain vocation, and that word is "calling."

Unfortunately, most people are not into their work near enough for it to even approach the "calling" level. According to a study by the employee research and consulting firm Towers Perrin,[12] only 17 percent of employees are highly engaged in their work. This means that the vast majority of us spend much of our time (about one-third of our lives in fact) engaged in activities that we either dislike or are essentially disinterested in. Investing so much time and energy in areas that yield little substantive return makes cultivating a life infused with meaning exceedingly difficult.

Not surprisingly, according to New York University business professor Dr. Amy Wrzesniewski and colleagues,[13] individuals who view their work as a calling are significantly happier than those who simply trudge through their workdays. Based on their study, Wrzesniewski places all workers in one of three groups:

- The "Job" group focuses almost exclusively on remuneration with little regard for fulfillment or pleasure.
- The "Career" group focuses on strategic advancement within the field and getting ahead.
- The "Calling" group works with an emphasis on personal fulfillment and the social import of what they do for work.

Not only was the Calling group happier than the others, they were found to have higher job satisfaction and even better physical health. Finally, one would think that the Calling group would be limited to those "do-gooders" in traditional helping fields (e.g., teacher, therapist, firefighter, etc.), but this was not always the case. As the authors write, "Within any occupation, one could conceivably find individuals with all three kinds of relations to their work...it is plausible that salespersons, medical technicians, factory workers, and secretaries could view their work as a Calling. Such people could love their work and think that it contributes to making the world a better place." Thus, we need necessarily to be in careers that are overtly and obviously altruistic to reap the benefits of having a calling.

Health Benefits of Living with Purpose and Meaning

We have seen how living with meaning and purpose can improve your mental outlook and sense of personal fulfillment, but it has significant physical health benefits as well. According to Michael T. Murray, MD,[14] variables related to living meaningful lives, like altruism and positive relationships, are "closely related to the ability to overcome life-threatening crises and disease...and maintain good health." More specifically, David Bennet,[15] Director of the Alzheimer's Disease Center at Rush University Medical Center in Chicago, and his colleagues conducted a seven-year study and determined that those who perceived their lives as less meaningful were *more than twice as likely* to develop Alzheimer's as compared to those who reported higher levels of meaning in their lives. And in perhaps the greatest test of resiliency, a different review of this same group found that, over a five-year period, those who lived with high levels of purpose and meaning were 57 percent less likely to die within a given time period when compared with those living with lower levels.

In other studies, living with a sense of purpose has been positively associated with a 30 percent reduced risk of heart attack as well as a significant increase in the likelihood of remaining heart attack free.[16] Finally, a strong sense of purpose has been correlated with higher amounts of HDL cholesterol (yes, that is the "good" kind), lower levels of the stress hormone cortisol, and, strange as it may seem, even a slimmer appearance.[16]

Our Essential Need for Meaning

So clearly meaning and purpose matter, a lot. But why? Earlier I mentioned Viktor Frankl. You may be broadly familiar with his story. But here is a very brief review: Frankl was a Jew living in Austria and a psychiatrist by profession. In 1942 he and his family were forced into the Theresienstadt concentration camp in Czechoslovakia. Leaving him behind, his wife and parents were eventually moved to different camps and ultimately perished while imprisoned. Over the course of three years, Frankl had been moved to several different camps himself but was finally liberated in 1945. He chronicled his time in the camps and his psycho-spiritual journey in the relatively short classic mentioned earlier, *Man's Search for Meaning*.

Many people who endure such ordeals do not like talking about them—it's simply too painful. But Frankl found a certain catharsis in discussing his life in the camps and was committed to making that time meaningful for both him and his future patients and, as he could not have known for sure at the time, much of the world.

One of the intriguing conclusions he came to amid the horrific circumstances was that even when it appears that everything has been stripped away from a human being, he maintains a degree of choice, even if the options from which to choose are extremely limited. Significantly, the decision that Frankl found most vital to his survival was the choice to extract meaning from his struggles and from his pain. To accomplish this he needed a purpose, a goal, a mission to make the pain *mean* something. For Frankl this was the only thing that made it bearable. He writes, "any attempt to restore a man's inner strength in the camp had first to succeed in showing him some future goal...Whenever there was an opportunity for it, one had to give them a why—an aim—for their lives, in order to strengthen them to bear the terrible *how* of their existence. Woe to him who saw no more sense in his life, no aim, no purpose, and therefore no point in carrying on. He was soon lost." (p. 98).

Frankl was so inspired by his observations regarding the need for meaning in life that he used the concepts as the basis for the development of a new school of psychotherapy, which he termed *logotherapy*. ("Logos" is an important and seminal Greek word with a variety of meanings including *idea*, *concept*, and *words*. It also signifies *meaning*, which is why Frankl chose it.) In a nutshell logotherapy is based on the premise that the primary motivation of human beings is to secure meaning from their worlds, and if they cannot or do not do so, mental anguish and neurosis will result. Logotherapy touched such a nerve and existing need that it eventually became known as the Third Viennese School of Psychotherapy, after Freud's "psychoanalysis" and Adler's "individual psychology."

Even those of us not in therapy or currently experiencing an existential crisis can often see how being directionless can greatly increase anxiety. Frankl coined the term "Sunday Neurosis" (not to be confused with Sundaynightitis which was coined by that equally esteemed thinker, Morales, and which will be discussed in a later chapter) to capture the experience that many people have when they are not at work, and lacking the structure, guidance, and meaning their jobs impart, they begin to view their lives as empty and purposeless.

Did you know that the fastest motorcycle in the world traveled at over 376 miles per hour? But here is the really important question: could it even keep from toppling over if it weren't moving? A motorcycle is a good illustrative metaphor. If it's guided in a certain direction with a certain amount of energy, it can travel with exceptional alacrity, economy, and velocity. But when it stops, when it no longer has intention or direction, it topples over.

According to Frankl and others, this is how we are wired to a large extent. This is why, as Buchholz intimated earlier, retirement is such a problem for so many seniors. If they don't replace their work with something else they find meaningful, they can find themselves stuck in a quicksand of aimless existence, passively watching time tick by and dreading every second.

This reminds me of a story of a woman living in ancient times who was searching for the meaning of life. She lived in a town that had a seaport and was told by the elders that she would find the meaning of life there. So each day she went to the port looking for the meaning of life, but all she found were ships filled with orphans displaced by a faraway war.

Not knowing what else to do, she began feeding, clothing, and taking care of the kids. Years went by and more and more children needing her care came, but she found no answers to her quest for meaning.

Decades later she was so immersed in continuing to take care of the children that she had forgotten her original search for the meaning of life. And as the story goes, that is when she found it.

The story can be interpreted in many ways, but I like to focus on how the doing of meaningful deeds, as opposed to waiting passively, is often the best route toward a fulfilling life. The meaning comes from the completion of worthwhile goals, and the two reinforce each other.

Dr. Steven Hobfall, head of the Behavioral Sciences Department at Rush University Medical Center in Chicago,[17] articulates key aspects of goal setting and how instrumental meaning can be. Hobfall believes three elements are crucial to the process: *commitment, flow,* and *vigor.* These three concepts are essentially by-products of meaning and are woven into the process of living resilience.

- *Commitment* comes from meaning and value. As we have seen, we won't commit fully unless the meaning level is high enough.
- *Flow* occurs when we are so *into* the act of manifesting what is of value that we become completely absorbed in the process.

- *Vigor* is the energy we can extract from the process, but remember it can only be sustained if the meaning level is high enough.

It is difficult to overstate the crucial role that *meaning* can play in the process of building our resiliency. Essentially, meaning is our core source of energy—the force that fuels all of the actions, both pleasant and unpleasant, that we must take to overcome whatever labyrinthine mess we find ourselves in so that we can emerge relatively intact. If resilience is the stretching of the rubber band, meaning dictates how far we're willing to go.

Meaning as Measuring Stick

Would you show up at your work or school stark-naked for a million dollars?

Your answer to this question says a lot about how important money is to you (and perhaps how often you work out). This question is part of a game that I, and others I'm sure, sometimes play with friends and family. You choose an outrageous activity (e.g., showing up to work naked, spending the night alone in New York City's Central Park, eating someone else's vomit, etc.) and offer an amount of money in order to do it. It's lots of fun, but it can also serve as a type of values clarification exercise. If you play it enough, you begin to see patterns in certain people's responses, and you realize what is and isn't important to them. My mother, for example, will rarely say yes to any of the activities—not because she is squeamish or prudish; it's just that money is not *that* important to her. My cousin on the other hand would agree to do almost anything for a million dollars (including only being able to say "crabby patties" for six months)— different people, different values.

The point here is that if you want to know how important something is to you, how much it really *means*, then reflect on what you are or are not willing to do or endure to achieve it. These do not have to be massive missions like scaling Mount Everest or standing in front of a tank in

Tiananmen Square. We can look at smaller and more mundane goals and gauge how much they really mean to us by what we are willing to do in the process of achieving them.

I once had a student whose actions baffled me until I applied this meaning measurement construct to his situation.

Tony the Liar

Tony was a young man of nineteen who came to me as part of a summer bridge program (a college preparation program for at-risk students) before his freshman year. He had struggled with the intense and compressed summer course work almost from the beginning. I brought him in for his midprogram counseling session and, to his credit, he was quick to hold himself accountable.

"I know what the problem is, Dr. M," he began. "I'm just *so* lazy."

When students admit their laziness, there is not much I can do. While the cause of the problem is clear, the solution is not, especially when there is limited time with which to work. As any teacher (or parent) knows, one can't make someone, anyone, go from lazy to hardworking. That is something he or she must do for him or herself. Even with all my years of study and work in this area, I am frustrated and at a loss working with these folks. If a student really is inherently lazy (which is rare but does happen) then my bag of tricks will have little if any effect.

Essentially, one of two related phenomena must occur to release this individual from his or her self-imposed prison of laziness. Either the individual must wait until (and if) he or she gets fed up with the fruits (or lack thereof) of being lazy. Or the individual encounters something so meaningful that inaction is no longer a desirable option. Then and only then will he or she be willing to modify behavior.

Back to Tony. Later on that day, as I was getting in my car to go home, he drove by in a shiny late-model pickup truck with the words "Tony's

Landscaping" emblazoned across the side in fancy green script. I waved him over and asked if the truck and business was his father's. (It was more than mere curiosity—to be honest I needed a new landscaper and thought I might be able to get a discount of some type.) To my surprise, it was not his father's business, but his!

I asked him when on Earth he had time to run a landscaping company. Not only was he only nineteen, but the summer college program began at nine thirty in the morning and ended at three, four days a week. He went on to tell me he had people working for him during the day, and he then joined them every afternoon from a quarter to four until it got dark at about nine o'clock, *and* he worked all day and evening Fridays as well as most weekends. I then looked at him with the most serious face I could muster and said, "Tony, you're a liar!"

He looked at me as if I had just told him I used to be a woman. "What are you talking about, Dr. M?" he replied. I said, "You told me you were lazy. Clearly you are not. You work twelve hours a day almost every day. If you're *lazy* then I'm king of the couch potatoes."

"Yeah, but that's different," he said.

"Really? Why?" I replied.

"Because I work to get money to pay for my car and go out and stuff. It's really imp—" He stopped himself there.

He was going to say it was really *important* to him, but he knew if he admitted that, then in essence he'd be saying school was *unimportant.*

It appeared that both he and I had misdiagnosed the problem. It was not his general and innate laziness but rather his *priorities* that were the root cause of his academic difficulties. Like many nineteen-year-olds, school was just not meaningful enough for him to expend the type of energy necessary. He didn't see the connection between school and what was personally important to him. Consequently he adopted a laissez-faire attitude toward academics while employing his real passion in his landscaping business.

One of the ways we can manufacture meaning is by focusing our energies on those whom we love. The world is full of people whose primary focus is others and who achieved greatness because of it.

In my research on academically successful poor students, one of the most common and powerful motivators is their desire to pay back their parents for all of their parents' sacrifices. This was especially true for the children of immigrants, who were well aware of all the struggles their parents endured without complaint so their children could have improved educational and financial opportunities. Often for these students, the idea of *not* taking advantage of these hard-won opportunities is tantamount to minimizing and dismissing all their parents had done. When these students wanted to quit, they remembered their parents' struggles and found the energy to move on. For them, justifying their parents' hardships was what was most meaningful.

Making it Work for You

According to my word processing program's thesaurus, two antonyms for the word *resilience* are *rigidity* and *defeatism.* I respectfully disagree with Mr. Gates and the other creators of Microsoft Word. If I could only choose one word as an antonym for resilience, it would be "powerlessness." The resilience process is one of personal empowerment, and as we've discussed throughout the chapter, there is no better fuel for our power than personal meaning. It's the *super-high-octane-ultra-unleaded* jet fuel of human motivation. But how do we cultivate, refine, and burn this fuel? To begin with we must be willing to engage in profound and honest introspection so as to unearth that which we really, truly, and deeply care about.

Identifying What We Truly Value and Why: An Exercise in Meaning

Thoughtfully and honestly engaging in the following values-clarification exercise will not only help reveal what is important to you but will also demonstrate *why* you should value and support these things in your daily life.

The following can be done individually or with a group. If you do it in a group setting, make certain you are completely at ease and comfortable with all the members. Even a slight reluctance to be completely candid when doing this exercise can greatly decrease its probative value.

Materials needed: Ten slips of paper or flashcards and a writing implement.

Procedure:

1. You will use the papers/cards to identify the items that are most important to you in the world. On each of the slips write one thing that is extremely, truly, deeply, and profoundly important to you. Do not worry about rating which is the most valuable, which is second, etc. Just get them all down. Take your time with this—do not rush. If you need to sleep on it, go ahead. These items could be anything—people, ideas, places, animals, objects, etc., but come up with ten of them, and make them somewhat *specific*. For example, instead of *family* write *children,* and instead of *work* write what you actually do (e.g., *helping people plan for retirement).*

2. Lay all ten slips of paper in front of you and contemplate how much each item means to you and why.

3. Then grab the one that is *least* meaningful among them, and put a "10" in the corner. Imagine what it would feel like to lose that item forever. Now crumple it up and toss it onto the ground. In doing this, imagine that by throwing it away, you *are* losing it *forever*. Really feel deeply what it might be like to no longer possess that item, and identify the emotions that arise in the process of losing it.

4. Repeat step three, this time putting a "9" on the next least important item. Then do "8" then "7"…each time choosing the item among those

remaining that is the next *least* important, until you are left with one slip of paper (which gets a "1").

As you gradually throw away your most valuable and meaningful items, contemplate the decisions you are making. What criteria are you using to make these choices? How does it feel to lose these items? Which items are particularly painful to lose? Why? Are there some that are surprisingly easy to discard? Why? Think deeply and honestly, reflecting on the choices you're making and, just as importantly, why.

(Note: This may get very difficult, but do your best to "get off the fence" and choose which are more valuable than others. "But they are all important!" is not a satisfactory response.)

5. At this point you should be left with one slip of paper, representing the thing in the world that is most valuable and meaningful to you. Think long and hard about what that is and precisely *how* it infuses your life with meaning. Think about what you'd be willing to *do* to cultivate and nurture the well-being and existence of this item. Think about what you'd be willing to *endure* to protect this item from harm—to keep it whole. Think about the lengths you'd go to keep from losing it.

6. Then crumple up that last piece of paper and toss it along with the rest. Think about how that feels. Are you left with a sense of anxiety, dread, anger, or despair? What would it really be like to lose that item? Would your life then be purposeless and empty? Really capture *how* that item is important to you; what it provides you.

7. Now think about what you would endure, give, or do to get those items back had you actually lost them. Is what you would give or do different for the last few items you held onto as compared to the first ones you discarded? How?

8. Now scoop up all of the papers from the ground. Unfold and/or smooth them out. As you are smoothening out the wrinkles imagine that you are now reclaiming these items. Feel the joy and relief. Be grateful you

have not yet lost them and think about what you'd be willing to do to minimize the likelihood that you would actually lose them in the future.

9. Place the slips in two rows (one through five on the top and six through ten on the bottom).

If done well this exercise can provide you with two gifts: (1) *What* is important to you and (2) *Why*.

- First, note that if you did the exercise right, items numbered one through five (your top row) are what is *most* meaningful and important to you. *Your primary job in life is to protect, cultivate, and serve those items.* (Talk about getting your money's worth! I just provided you with your personalized life's purpose!) The values you place on these items are what will drive you to endure and overcome life's seemingly unrelenting challenges.

- Second, notice how painful it was to "lose" these important items. Feel both the initial sense of loss and the relief you felt when you got them back. You got to experience a rare phenomenon: having something valuable taken from you but getting it right back.

Though brief and artificial, this can be a powerful reminder of why these things are so valuable.

〜

Now that you know what really matters to you, you can tap reserves of energy by connecting the transcendence of your particular crisis to the well-being or cultivation of these invaluable items, people, or ideas.

Creating Eudaemonic Well-Being

Earlier we briefly discussed the work of Ryan and Deci and how these researchers emphasize that eudaemonic well-being involves a focus on *process* rather than *outcome*. These researchers go on to explore a model of eudemonia that is grounded in self-determination theory and consists of four basic motivational concepts. Of these there are two that I believe are especially relevant to our desire to use meaning to facilitate resilience.

The first is their advice to pursue *intrinsic* goals for their own sake (e.g., personal growth, physical health, and enhancing the community) rather than *extrinsic* goals (e.g., fame, wealth, image, and power), which rely heavily on the approval and perceptions of others. The second is the value they place on maximizing consciousness in our daily activities and acting with enhanced self-awareness.

The first tenant is basically telling us to be the captains of our own ships. To think about every decision we make and to ask ourselves whether the motivation is primarily coming from our outer or inner worlds. The second is reminding us to live consciously and to remain aware of the implications of our actions, thoughts, and emotions. In other words to minimize the amount of time we sleepwalk through life.

Those who live fulfilling lives spend the majority of their time being guided by their inner worlds and are less concerned with external validation. They are consistently aware of not just what they are doing, but *why* they are doing it. These focuses create a context where, succeed or fail, they are living life and making decisions based on their own terms. This has the added benefit of minimizing regret and resentment even if things go wrong...Hey, at least it was *your* decision.

To help get a sense of where you stand now and to keep these values front and center, here are some questions to ask yourself in regard to the choices you're making about your life and how you spend the brief time you're allotted on Earth. As always deep thought and absolute honesty are crucial. As you ponder each question think about how your life's meaning can be enhanced by paying homage to your inner guide and maximizing your awareness levels.

- Do I do things primarily for recognition or because they are meaningful to me?
- When in public is my attention primarily focused on how I am being perceived by others or on being my most authentic self?
- Do I choose to be around certain people because I like how I feel about myself when I'm with them or because I like how I think *they* feel about me?
- When making an important decision, am I primarily concerned with how I will feel about it or with how I think it will be perceived by others?
- Do I commit actions then wonder, *What the hell was I thinking about?*
- Am I frequently on "autopilot," acting without much thought?
- Which of the following is my primary motivation in life: *fear, caring, self-expression,* or *insecurity?*

If you find that you're not crazy about your answers, don't fret. Most of us spend lots of time being guided by the outside worlds and are rarely even aware of it. The purpose of pondering these questions is not necessarily to get you to completely change gears by tomorrow morning, but rather to facilitate your awareness as to what's really guiding you. If you can begin to move toward making decisions based on your inner values rather than fear and insecurity, you will be in a much better position to add meaning to your life.

CHAPTER 4:
ACTION

"So, you think we'll have shade by lunchtime?"

"D̲amn! What the *hell* am I going to do now?"

Any of us who have ever uttered this fateful interjection and nine-word question know the weeks and months that followed significantly altered the trajectory of our lives—either for better or worse. This question is usually asked at critical turning points in our lives when faced with trauma, loss, or some other form of crises. In response we all *did* something (even if that something was nothing), but the psycho-emotional factors that dictated the choice of action, the "behind the scenes" forces, are really the critical players here. Yes, in the end it is what we do that makes the difference, but to maximize our resilience capacity, we must remember how implicitly and fully *action* is linked with *acceptance* and *meaning*.

The reality is, despite your mother's berating, you *usually* do *think* before you act (that is, unless you are the victim of one of those nasty emotional-high hijackings we discussed earlier). However, the quality and origins of the thoughts that precede and guide our actions is rarely given its fair due.

Quality Plans Based in Reality

If we can think of *Acceptance* and *Meaning* as huge rungs on a metaphorical ladder (see figure five below) that allow us to see as much and as clearly as possible, the *Action* phase is what we *do* based on our better vantage points and newly *enhanced vision*. Assuming this sequence is followed, the action now becomes *strategic.*

At the risk of overdosing on metaphors, think of the trauma from which we are attempting to bounce back as placing us in a deep hole. Essentially, resilient people climb out of the hole using this ladder. The ladder ensures their actions are made up of highly effective tactics and have enough force to overcome whatever challenges may be in the way.

Figure 5: Resilience Ladder

Think about the value that comes with designing action plans based on "good intel." This is why military campaigns risk so many lives and spend so much time on reconnaissance missions. Without understanding and insights into what the enemy is doing and what it means, effective action plans are difficult to design. Consequently, it is rare to find resilient people who are erratic, impulsive, and capricious. There simply are not many of them. Virtually every resilient person I have studied could be described not just as a planner but as a deeply *strategic* planner. They think long and hard about the best approaches to an issue before actually *doing* anything. And often "best" is derived from both accepting that which cannot be changed—regardless of how sour it may taste going down—as well as focusing on that which is most meaningful and beneficial at a particular point in time.

Once we have enhanced our vision and can see truth with clarity, we can then enter the action phase with the required confidence that what we do will indeed have the desired impact. This confidence in our own self-efficacy is perhaps the most commonly cited characteristic of resilient individuals.

Self-efficacy can be defined as our belief in our ability to successfully achieve the results we desire. And according to the research, the more genuine and robust our belief in our agency, the more action we will commit and the more likely it is that we will be successful.

Pray at the Altar of Self-Efficacy

Anyone really serious about resilience must add a new god to his/her life, namely the god of self-efficacy. Self-efficacy must become a life mantra so embedded in our world view that it becomes automatic and reflexive. Like a god for a religious person, self-efficacy is where resilient people turn when they are at a loss as to how to proceed.

Figure six below identifies the three primary pillars that promote effective action (assuming one is acting in a strategic manner based on acceptance of reality and an appropriately meaningful belief system). Action induced by self-efficacy is an umbrella concept that directly informs, in one way or another, virtually every aspect of how resilient people respond to crisis. Furthermore, two of self-efficacy's most important offspring, *persistence* and the ability to *delay gratification,* will be explored in great detail in this chapter. These crucial approaches to action are made possible in large part by the existence of high levels of self-efficacy.

The overarching importance and value of self-efficacy for resilience has been well established, but its source and degree of pliability are more mysterious. According to the father of self-efficacy research, Stanford University psychological researcher Albert Bandura,[1] self-efficacy derives from four primary sources of information: *performance accomplishments, vicarious experience, verbal persuasion,* and *physiological states* (emotional arousal). Briefly looking at each through the particular lens of resilience promotion will allow us to better understand how self-efficacy and the resulting action are manufactured.

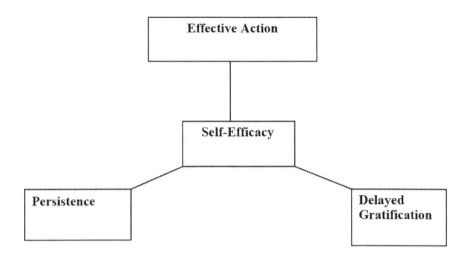

Figure 6: Pillars of Effective Action

Performance accomplishments are the most powerful and effective means of building self-efficacy. It essentially refers to using past accomplishments as evidence/encouragement for future success. When faced with doubt and circumspection, resilient people often "Google" their memory banks, identifying analogous instances when their efforts have paid off. As the individual builds up an ample amount of success evidence, even new "failures" and/or obstacles do not corrupt the individual's belief in him or herself. Negative experiences that are then overcome provide even more evidence of the potency of his or her self-efficacy, thus strengthening it.

Through his research Bandura also found that even *dissimilar* challenges can benefit from previous accomplishments. In other words even when the personal success was in a completely different context, the personal success is transferable to the present challenge. For example, if you are doubting the value of studying for an important exam, you can use the hard work and resulting success you may have put into training for a marathon as evidence of your ability. This is important, because it means you can gain real confidence even in an area to which you are new and inexperienced (as long as you have a somewhat analogous situation to draw from).

To explore the potential use of each of the four self-efficacy building blocks, let's use the common setback of being let go (OK, let's keep it real—*fired*) from a job and searching for another. You've now sent out dozens of résumés and cover letters and are hearing nothing back from prospective employers. If you can think back *vividly* to times when you did receive callbacks, and ultimately job offers, then you can use these memories as bits of evidence supporting the wisdom, and ultimate payoff, of your efforts. If this is the first time you have had to seek out and secure a job on your own (and thus lack this particular success in your past) then you will have to identify a comparable success from which to draw confidence. For example, maybe initially you didn't get into the colleges of your choice but eventually did. Though not identical these are comparable enough that one will provide belief and motivation for the other.

Remember, the value here is not simply the belief that is generated, it is that this belief will encourage you to continue to put forth the effort necessary (in this case continuing to send cover letters and résumés) to eventually achieve your objective.

Vicarious experience is another useful, though less somewhat impactful, way of building self-efficacy. As the name suggests, vicarious experience involves learning from the actions of others and viewing these others as models. Maybe you cannot recall any incidents from your own life that truly convince you that continuing to send our employment materials will make a difference. In this case reading about or observing *others* who have secured employment in this fashion can make the difference. This accounts for the value and popularity of inspirational stories, role models, and cautionary tales as well as the common rhetorical question—*Hey, why not me, gosh darn it?*

We should remember though that while we can get inspired by the experiences of others, we believe more in what we've experienced ourselves. This is why I sometimes cringe when entering inner-city schools and observe the "inspirational" slogans that wallpaper many of the classrooms. "Reach for the stars," "You can be anything if you put your mind to it," and "All you have to do is believe" are not inherently bad messages, but without any track record of success (and amid a real lack of physical and psycho-emotional resources), they can not only ring hollow but actually encourage students to blame their parents and themselves for their plights: "They didn't make it—I guess my parents just didn't believe enough." As with anything else, go down this road with a critical eye.

Verbal persuasion comes not from experiencing past success or watching others negotiate similar obstacles but rather from being *told* we can do it. Strategic encouragement and support from people whom we respect and admire, along with a sincere belief in the validity of their words, can go a long way in helping us believe earnestly in ourselves. Additionally, it should be noted that the more we revere the individual providing the encouragement, especially in relation to the particular challenge being faced, the more impactful their words would be. (This is why compliments from our parents often lack impact—they usually love everything about us no matter what. When I tell my daughter she is beautiful she says, "Oh, Dad, that doesn't count. You *have* to say that.") Thus our frustrated job seeker would respond more to a human resources expert or headhunter telling her she should persist rather than a close friend or family member. It is often true that the right words at the right time from the right person can make all the difference. However, do keep in mind the work of Carol Dweck we discussed earlier—certain types of praise, particularly praise focused on areas we can directly influence, appear to be most efficacious.

Physiological states refer to the degree of anxiety connected with the challenge and how that anxiety (or lack thereof) can impact the degree to which we feel we can impact a given situation. In order to maximize self-efficacy we should attempt to place ourselves in optimal emotional states. For most of us, this would be calmness and serenity; however, others may feel more powerful and engaged with a modicum of stress and angst added to the mix.

Our particular physiological state is most significant when we are in the midst of critical decision making points. For example, our job seeker may get "faklempt" and ultimately fed up when she gets a "thanks, but no thanks" notice from a prospective employer about whom she felt particularly optimistic, but that moment is not a good time to decide if continued effort is warranted. That decision should be made once she has acquired a sense of emotional equilibrium. The lesson here is to be aware of how a *temporary* emotional state may affect decision making that has *lasting impact.*

Like many things in life, building self-efficacy is more a matter of degree than "yes, I have it" or "no, I don't" (as we will discover when we discuss its close cousin *internal locus of control*). There are situations where we are virtually 100 percent confident that our actions will indeed achieve the effect we desire (e.g., the color socks we put on in the morning, or how we choose to greet the first person we see at work, etc.), and there are other areas where we know our actions, no matter how sincere, will have no impact (e.g., our natural hair color, or our ability to hold our breath for two hours, etc.), but most of the solutions to crises we desire fall into a more gray area, an area that we have *partial* or *possible* influence over. Consequently, as we will see, the goal becomes to *extend* the reach of our self-efficacy, not world domination.

While self-efficacy refers to our confidence in our abilities, the related belief that *we* hold sway over our destinies, as opposed to some outside force, is what well-known researcher and psychologist Julian Rotter[2] referred to as an *internal locus of control.* Essentially, Rotter's theory is that people can be categorized as having either an *internal* or *external* locus of control (*locus* being Latin for location or place and *control* being English for, well, control). Those with an internal locus of control truly believe, deep in their bones, that they control what happens in their lives—that what they are, get, and have are direct fruits of their action (or inaction). In contrast those with an external locus of control believe that *others* (society, teachers, government, parents, fate, etc.) control what they are, get, and have.

In other words *overriding worldview* =

Internal Control:	**External Control:**
What I am, do, and have is because of **me**	What I am, do, and have is because of **others**

No Excuse for Poor Excuses

One way to detect external thinking is by looking at patterns of excuse making. Not only do those with external thinking emphasize excuses more, but their excuses tend to stress variables *beyond* their control (e.g., *the dog ate my homework,* or, more appropriate for these modern times, *the dog ate my flash drive*).

In thinking of these concepts and the homework-eating dogs. I can't help but recall some of the crazy and often humorous externally based excuses my own students sometimes bring to me for why they don't have their work or did poorly on an exam. There ought to be some medical investigation done, because the percentage of grandparents who die spikes every semester during finals week!

As a special treat, I have included a list of the top ten worst excuses my students have given me for poor academic performance over twenty years of teaching. Drumroll please...

10. I guess you don't like me.

9. The test wasn't fair because we had to know too much.

8. The font was too small.

7. My cousin had tickets to Beyoncé, and I just *had* to go.

6. I was disturbed by the birds chirping outside.

5. It was too hot. It was too cold. (two different students after the same exam in the same room!)

4. My horoscope said I'd fail.

3. I was having my period. (Note: Amazingly, this young woman's menstrual cycle seemed to kick into high gear every time we had an exam or a paper was due!)

2. I was waiting in line all night for the new iPhone   .
   And the number one absolute worst excuse in two decades of teaching...

I. How could I have failed the exam? The girl in front of me is really smart!

OK, I made that last one up, but I think you get the picture. Resilience requires that we limit the amount of time and energy we place on outside forces so that we can focus in on that which we can directly influence.

Several points here before we move on. First, it is difficult to ignore the religious and political connotations of Rotter's theory. When teaching the concepts to undergraduates, I often get a question like, "So, if you believe in God and that He is ultimately controlling everything, then you must have an external locus of control, right? So, Dr. Morales, are you saying that in order to be resilient we must not believe in God?" Even though I have been asked this question several times, it still throws me for a bit of a loop. Part of me wants to respond with, "Go ask your parents!" But that would be an intellectual cop out. What I do say is that if one believes in God, then it depends on how one interprets God's existence and influence. If one truly believes there is a God micromanaging every facet of our lives, then the supposition of the student's question is indeed accurate. That belief system is not consistent with an internal locus of control. However, based on my observations, I do not believe that most religious people hold onto this view of God as a micromanager. Most live in accordance with the well-known words of Benjamin Franklin: "God helps those who help themselves." However, it is true that those who deeply believe in destiny, or that some things are "meant to be" and others are not, are less likely to have internal loci of control.

Similarly, it is easy to couch an internal locus of control as a more conservative/free-market, political-economic philosophy, and an external as more socialistic and liberal. This again is an oversimplification. An internal locus of control does not mean picking yourself up by your bootstraps and doing everything by yourself. It means believing that you should and can exploit (in a positive sense) all of the resources at your disposal. If those resources (e.g., government and social services) are not available, then there are fewer tools with which one can work. Consequently, the internal/external dichotomy does not correspond neatly with the conservative/liberal one.

The bottom line is that in terms of building the capacity to be resilient, whether done consciously or subconsciously, adopting too much of an external locus of control can be disastrous. Think about it. If you really believe that others (or external events) control your life, then like Minnesota in January, you'll eventually become frozen, not able, willing, or eager to do anything. Why would you? If events are really out of your hands, then why exert any energy at all? Just sit at home, watch *Dancing with the Stars*, and snack on tortilla chips. Fully internalizing an external locus of control is disempowering to the point of impotence. Like a thief in the night, it robs us of both the confidence and energy needed to act in promotion of our potential resilience.

Keep in mind that our stances toward locus of control are often operating without us giving them much overt thought. The potential of subconscious or semiconscious adherence to external locus of control thinking is not to be taken lightly.

Many of you reading this are probably thinking to yourselves—*Dugh! Of course we must believe that our actions influence our lives. I don't need anyone to tell me that.* But like many simple but important concepts, pulling this concept out of the closet and critically examining it in a well-lit room can not only help us see what is really going on but provide reinforcement as well. Furthermore, most of us would never acknowledge outright, "I don't believe that my actions directly influence my world." But, we often live and react to crisis with this very notion as our predominant guide. And even worse, we think it's the norm.

Don't believe me? Think about all the people who spend significant portions of their income on lottery tickets, casino gambling, and meeting their bookies in the backs of dive bars. What is that if not belief in external forces (i.e., luck) rather than what we can influence directly? And I'd bet (pun intended) that even the nongamblers among us often cross our fingers, knock on wood, and toss loose change in a fountain, all in attempts to shape our reality.

This reminds me of the time a few years ago after my mother-in-law had a minor stroke and we were all visiting her in the hospital. In the room were both my wife and kids as well as my sister-in-law and her two daughters. There was a wheelchair in the room, and being the juvenile adult I often am, I began playing with it. I sat in the chair and whirled around a bit and started smiling.

My sister-in-law (who is a lovely person, by the way) looked at me as if I were dangling one of her children over a hotel balcony. "What are you doing!" she shrieked. "You're not supposed to sit in a wheelchair unless you need to! If you keep doing that you'll end up in one permanently!" Knowing how superstitious she could be, I decided to push her buttons a bit harder. "Actually," I said, twirling some more, "it's kind of fun. I hope I do end up in a wheelchair." She went apoplectic, practically yanking me from the chair.

She really believed that my sitting in a wheelchair and acting like a fool would indeed increase the likelihood of my being in an accident and ending up unable to walk. And most people would think that *I* was the crazy one. I tell this story not to make light of the serious challenges of being wheelchair bound, but to show how deeply ingrained our external locus of control tendencies can be.

Often the tendency toward external thinking exhibits itself in less obvious ways. The dating and romantic relationship landscape can teach us much about this topic. According to a Marist College poll[3,] 73 percent of Americans believe in the concept of soul mates. And tellingly, younger Americans are more likely than older Americans to believe that two people are destined to be together. The potentially comforting concepts of soul mates and destiny are firmly rooted in external locus of control thinking. Generally, the more we believe our lives to be fated, the less we believe in our ability to directly influence them.

The above research finding regarding age and belief in fate corresponds with my own observations. I have noticed that people in their twenties often talk of romantic destiny and soul mates and place less emphasis on the more practical need to get out there and meet as many potential mates as possible. "Why should I?" they often say—when we find each other, we find each other." They might even start signing Billy Joel's "You can't hurry love." However, single people I know in their late thirties and early forties take much more practical and proactive approaches to changing their relationship statuses. A reluctantly divorced friend of mine recently compared finding a new mate to sales and cold calling. As he put it, "It's a numbers game. The more I put myself out there, the more women I'll meet, and the more likely they'll be a match." While the former approach may be more romantic than the latter, it is also more ineffectual.

I also find it telling that younger people would believe more in fate from a maturity standpoint. Perhaps we can correlate maturity with an internal locus of control and lack of maturity with an external. Speaking for myself I know that when I was younger, I was more inclined to believe that luck and fortune were the primary determinants in people's lives. But accompanying my gray hair has been an appreciation for, and belief in, the significance of what people actually do.

In contrast to our lottery devotees, those with internal loci of control are able to continually put forth the massive amounts of energy necessary to influence change because they believe those efforts will indeed pay off. Now, notice I changed the word "control" to "influence." I think this makes much more sense. As we've discussed, the truth is we rarely, if ever, *control* anything or anyone (any of us with children know how true this is).

But we can and do influence much more than we think. And that is the key to expanding our resilience capacity—maximizing the degree to which we truly believe we influence outcome.

Going back to the academic world, an overriding belief system shared by college students with external locus of control thinking is that teachers *give* grades (as opposed to its opposite view, students *earn* grades). I often hear students discussing papers or exams they receive back, and most of the time if it's a low grade, they'll say something like, "Damn, *he gave* me a D!" But when it is a high grade, they'll say, "Look, *I* got an A!" Essentially, they want credit for the good but don't want to take responsibility for the bad.

Resilient students believe deep in their bones that grades are reflections of what they do or don't do. To think in any other way takes power and influence away and turns them into pawns, vulnerable to the whims of others and their environments.

To illustrate how differences in thoughts surrounding locus of control can affect action and eventual outcome, let's look at two hypothetical students. Desmond and Katrina both have a big math test coming up on Monday. Both have earned Ds on their previous exam and desperately want to improve their grades. They both view their math professor, Dr. Chin, as a bit cold and impersonal and somewhat intimidating. Notice that all of the contextual factors are identical for Desmond and Katrina. BUT— Desmond has an external locus of control, and Katrina an internal.

Let's set the stage: It's Thursday evening, and they're both eating dinner with a bunch of friends in the dining hall. A mutual friend of theirs, Bobby, comes by and asks if they're going to the huge fraternity party off campus that night. If we could climb into their brains during the two to three critical seconds during which they are deciding on their responses (their "response-ability" time), the following is what we might see.

Inside Desmond's Brain

Man, my math professor, Dr. Chin, hates me anyway. I know she's going to give me a D because she always does. It really doesn't matter what I do, I'm still going to get that D. I studied for like a half hour straight for the last test and *still* got a D, so what's the use? If I'm meant to get an A, I will. I'll just leave it up to fate.

Desmond's Answer

"Yeah, Bobby, I coming. What time does it start?"

Inside Katrina's Brain

I really need to bring my math grade up and don't have much time this weekend. I can't prepare the way I did last time, or I will probably get another D. But if I put in two hours tonight and finish the review questions then see Dr. Chin during her early morning office hours to go over them tomorrow, I can then spend Saturday in the math lab with a tutor. Then I should really be able to tackle that exam. I'll then be able to go out Saturday night instead.

Katrina's Answer

"Nah Bobby, I've got some stuff to do, you guys have fun though."

Here we can see that while both students are at about the same academic level (starting point), the likelihood that they will put forth enough energy to do well on the next exam is completely dependent on what they believe influences their grades. Desmond, with his external locus of control, believes it is his professor's dislike of him that will determine his grade and that his past performance dictates his future performance. He's given up on the potential of his own effort to provide him with any results. For Desmond it's about others.

Katrina, on the other hand (with her internal locus of control), really thinks that she can take steps to get a better grade on her next exam, and consequently she takes those steps. She doesn't think about whether or not Dr. Chin likes her, and she's even going to see Dr. Chin early in the morning to get help. She doesn't focus on what she has done in the past but rather focuses on the future, and most importantly, based on that focus, she takes action.

As seen above, academic performance is an area where the causes and effects of locus of control can be easily measured. The phenomenon of students suffering from external loci of control is common enough that it has spurred its own term within the educational lexicon, "learned helplessness." According to special education teacher Carmen Reyes,[4] learned helplessness refers to a "Lack of perceived control over their (the students') own behavior and the environmental events; (the belief that) one's own actions cannot lead to success."

Let us stop to think about how potentially debilitating this belief can be. Imagine walking around thinking, *No matter what I do, no matter how much effort I exert, success will elude me.* It is the perfect self-fulfilling prophecy storm. Learned helplessness is particularly prevalent for students growing up on low socioeconomic environments where hardship, adversity, and stress conspire to produce a seemingly endless torrent of frustration and perpetual disappointment. Within such a framework, it is not difficult to see how belief in one's self-efficacy can quickly erode, especially from the already seemingly powerless context of childhood.

Learned helplessness and external loci of control are so pernicious in large part because they are sneaky little buggers. As we've discussed often those suffering from these limiting beliefs are thoroughly unaware of their affliction. I have observed this sad occurrence firsthand and all too often. Once these individuals lose their belief in themselves, it is very difficult for them to find it again, but not impossible.

Oscar's Story

In thinking about this phenomenon, a student named Oscar immediately came to mind. Oscar was a bright, hardworking, twenty-year-old undergraduate who at one point was thoroughly beaten down by life and all but completely bereft of any sense of conviction that what he did would make any difference at all.

Oscar's mother was a fifteen-year-old heroin addict and drug dealer when she had him and wasn't sure who the father was. Upon revealing her pregnancy, she was summarily kicked out of her home. A few weeks later, she was arrested for possession, prostitution, and intent to distribute narcotics and sentenced to juvenile lockup. While they transferred her to a local hospital for the actual birth, once Oscar was born, his mother was taken right back to prison. She was in and out of prison for the first eight years of Oscar's life, so he spent much of his childhood under the "supervision" of a reluctant guardian: his aunt.

Oscar spent a good deal of his childhood alone. His aunt worked the night shift at a hotel and slept most of the day. While Oscar was an infant, he would stay with a neighbor until his aunt returned from work. At about age four, in order to save money, she kept him home alone, and only had the neighbor "check in on him" periodically. He was basically on his own and spent much of his time watching television.

Perhaps in large part due to his excessive isolation, Oscar did not start talking until he was about three and even then rarely spoke multiple word sentences. Adding to his challenges, because his aunt had "other things on her mind," Oscar was not registered for school until five months *after* his sixth birthday.

About a year and a half later, his mother finally returned to get him, and the two moved into a small one-room apartment. However, her continued drug use, promiscuity, and frequent absences had Oscar raising her as much as she him. He spent endless nights comforting his mother after a breakup or when she couldn't get her hands on her drug of choice. He also recalls that when she was with a man she liked or was high, she had little use for him and would actually belittle his efforts to garner her attention. "Don't be such a pest." was one of her favorite rebuffs to his appeals.

Oscar was quiet in school and kept to himself. He was polite, worked hard, and was diligent about getting his homework done but still struggled academically. In retrospect he can now see how his unsettled home life must have subsumed much of his emotional and cognitive energy. But at the time it just manifested itself as frustration and the convincing belief that he is "just stupid." Furthermore, the lack of supervision and attention at home meant virtually no help with homework, and attendance at a parent-teacher conference was nothing more than a fantasy.

At age nine Oscar was diagnosed with a learning disability. To this day he is not certain exactly what the diagnosis was, but what he does know is that he only met with a doctor briefly, and the next thing he knew he was being pulled out of his classes for "special help." For this he was ridiculed by other students, and his view of himself as "damaged" and "pathetic" was further entrenched.

However dismal things seemed, Oscar was not without dreams. As early as he could remember, Oscar held a secret fantasy for his future, an ideal so farfetched and outrageous that he was often reluctant to even reveal it to himself. He wanted to be the opposite of everything he saw around him. He saw poverty and wanted wealth. He saw anxiety and sought calm. He lived with instability and craved consistency. And perhaps most of all, he wanted respect, both from others and himself.

All of these desires culminated in one image, that of a "businessman." And not just a businessman but one with a "shiny black briefcase." Oscar knew next to nothing about business or what business people actually did, but the image of himself in a suit and holding a briefcase brought rare smiles to his usually sullen face. (Interestingly, Oscar is not the only inner-city youth I've interviewed who fantasized about playing the role of "businessman." There seems to be something especially alluring about this concept for those who feel marginalized by mainstream society)

Oscar's dismally low regard for himself as a student remained. He remembers working hard but it never seeming to pay off. And while he did well enough to squeak through a low-rated high school, the entire time refusing to participate in any special-education programs, he began his community college education with deeply held doubts about his ability to perform and live the life he profoundly desired.

In Oscar's description of the start of his college career, we can see how close he is to fully internalizing his life's struggles and interpreting those challenges as definitive proof of his personal impotence. Essentially, he is in the precipice of a virtually incurable case of "learned helplessness."

> After my first few grades I was just like, here we go again. My papers had so much red on them it was like a crime scene…I remember getting home and looking at all I had to do, and I was like, what's the use? Who am I kidding? I can't be a businessman—I can't even get through remedial English!…I had all this stuff to do, exams and papers, and I just said forget it! I remember I was sitting at the kitchen table with all my books and stuff in front of me, and I just swept them off of the table and into the garbage. I was done…a minute later my mother walked into the kitchen and saw the books in the garbage. She looked at them, looked at me, and continued to the fridge for a beer.

Can we really blame Oscar for giving up? If anyone has a legitimate excuse for giving up and giving in, it's the Oscars of the world. Can't we almost say that Oscar's lack of self-efficacy is *legitimate*, that it's *warranted* given how he grew up? Probably. But given the topic of this book, we know, or at least hope, that Oscar will be able to turn things around.

Oscar dropped out that semester and just sort of hung out for several months. He tried halfheartedly to get a job, walking around and looking for "Help Wanted" signs, but nobody seemed to be hiring. He spent New

Year's Eve alone in his apartment (his mother was "sleeping out" again) and described that night as the "worst of his life."

> I felt like I was stuck in a bad place, not really a nightmare, less dramatic than that. Just a crappy, miserable place and that no matter what I would be stuck right there. I looked at my future and could no longer see myself as a businessman or really anything more than what I was. A broke, learning-disabled, misfit of a loser.

A few weeks later Oscar found himself walking past the community college he had briefly attended and ran into a math instructor of his, one of the few Oscar actually had liked. The instructor asked Oscar what had happened to him and why he stopped coming to class. Oscar replied with a simple, "I don't know. Things have been sort of messed up."

They talked for a bit, and the instructor suggested that Oscar meet with one of the counselors in the advising department to see what his options were, and even gave him the name of a particular one, Marie, who he said was exceptionally good.

Oscar wrote down the name perfunctorily, having no inclination to ever actually go to see her. *What's the use?* he thought. But as the professor walked away, he turned around and said, "By the way, I *will* check with Marie and make sure you went to see her." *Damn!* Oscar thought. *Now I actually have to go.*

To Oscar's surprise the counselor began the meeting not by looking at his transcript or reprimanding him for leaving school without officially withdrawing. Instead she wanted to hear his life story. So at first reluctantly, and then with a surprising sense of relief, it all came tumbling out of him, starting with his birth while his mother was incarcerated and culminating with his utterly miserable New Year's Eve realizations.

Upon completion of his story, the counselor did something that Oscar would not have predicted in a hundred years: she reached out her arm and asked if she could shake his hand. Startled, Oscar asked, "Why?" The counselor smiled and said, "Because you are a truly amazing person. The fact that you are here, right now, in my office, is nothing short of remarkable. I know it's selfish, but I want to shake your hand with the hope that maybe, just maybe, some of that magic just might rub off on *me*."

At first Oscar thought she was messing with him but quickly realized she wasn't. The two had a long conversation about how far he had traveled, how he had transcended the tough circumstances of his upbringing, and the remarkable nature of his spirit. Oscar couldn't help but believe her sincerity. *Why would she lie?* And gradually he began to feel better about who he was and what he'd managed to accomplish.

She ended the session by advising him to celebrate his finely honed survival skills and to remember that if he continued to put forth the effort and fight the way he was, those skills and attitude could take him where he wanted to go.

She scheduled a time for them to meet again a week later, and to his own surprise, Oscar actually kept his appointment. At his request she agreed to set aside the issue of his learning disability (a diagnosis Oscar didn't fully buy) for the semester with the promise they would revisit it if necessary, depending on how he did this time around. She told Oscar that the only way to get his GPA back up to par would be to retake the exact classes he had previously dropped/failed.

Once they were done with the registration, Marie then asked him a critical question, one that Oscar himself had been contemplating: "Oscar, what will you do differently this time around?" He thought about the question and about their long discussion and the conclusions they had come to together and replied, "I'll work hard, and when I am feeling doubts as to whether or not I can really do it, I'll think back to all that I've survived and done to get to this point, and then I'll work a bit harder."

She looked at him and smiled.

With the assistance of writing tutors and study groups, Oscar passed all of his classes that semester. He didn't get As, but he passed with solid Bs and Cs. He made it a habit to keep a notebook with his daily tasks, and at Marie's direction religiously checked off those he completed.

At the end of the semester, he went to Marie and proudly shared his grades. She told him to hold up his daily task notebook in one hand and his grades in the other. She then said, "Oscar, remember, this [she pointed to the notebook] caused that [she pointed to the grades]. You did it, again."

By the time Oscar got to me and shared his story, he no longer wanted to be a businessman. He was thinking of being a teacher and then maybe a guidance counselor. The optimism and energy he exuded, as well as his solid 3.0 grade point average, left little doubt in my mind he would be successful in whatever path he chose.

As in Oscar's case, another way to look at the external/internal continuum is to view it as going from powerless to powerful (see figure seven). For the chess aficionados among us, think of the external side as indicative of being a pawn, almost completely at the mercy of all the other pieces. While being at the internal side is tantamount to being a queen, able to move virtually anywhere.

Figure seven comes from a self-diagnostic survey included below. Our first goal is to see where we are on the scale, and our second is to move to the right.

External 20------------10------------0-------------10------------20 Internal
Powerless--Powerful
Pawn--Queen

Figure 7

If you are uncertain as to where you are on the internal/external continuum, the self-diagnostic survey below may help provide some clarification. Keep in mind that while your final score is not the definitive indicator of where you are, it can serve as one tool to consider.

Locating Your Locus Self- Survey

Let's locate your locus. Take the following brief quiz. Put a "1" if the statement *does not* describe you, put a "2" if the statement *describes you somewhat*, and put a "3" if it is *highly descriptive* (1= not descriptive, 2= somewhat descriptive, 3= highly descriptive).

IMPORTANT: To get value from this, you must be HONEST. Provide responses that are true for you, *not* responses you *wish* were true.

----

1. How much work I do seems to have little influence on my career. _____
2. Very rarely do I give up, even when I face significant roadblocks. _____
3. When I have a difficult problem, I often cross my fingers and hope for solutions. _____
4. I believe that I can find a solution to almost any problem. _____
5. I think my childhood is the biggest factor in determining who I am now. _____
6. If I eat well and exercise, I'll be able to live a long and healthy life._____
7. I believe in fate and that most outcomes are preordained. _____
8. I don't believe in luck at all. Effort and persistence produce success. _____

9. The government controls most of our lives and creates or eliminates opportunity. _____

10. I'm not a big believer in fate—I think we create our own outcomes. _____

11. I usually give up and give in when I hit a roadblock in my life. _____

12. When I begin a diet, I know that I will stick to it and lose weight in the end. _____

13. Luck is a very important factor for successful people. _____

14. The later I stay at work, the more I will eventually earn. _____

15. Events that occur are meant to be, and those that don't are not. _____

16. As long as I have enough time to prepare, I can do well at almost any task. _____

17. How much a supervisor likes me is an important factor in my eventual professional success. _____

18. I believe that if I set goals and meet objectives, I will almost always be successful. _____

19. Students who get good grades usually don't have to study very much. _____

20. Whatever political parties and politicians are in office do not affect my ability to be successful. _____

Scoring:

A. Add up your scores for the odd numbered statements and put your total here: _____

B. Add up your scores for the even numbered statements and put your total here: _____

C. Find the difference between the two numbers: _____

D. Check "External" if your odd score is higher, and check "Internal" if your even score is higher. External _____ or Internal _____

E. (Final Score) Your answer to letter C _____ and D, either External _____ or Internal _____

External = You have an external locus of control
Internal = You have an internal locus of control
The higher your number the stronger your locus of control is (external or internal)
External 20------------10------------0-------------10-------------20 Internal
Powerless--Powerful
Pawn---Queen

Think not only about where you ended up on the scale, but reflect on the *why*. Then use the "5 Step Activity Plan" in the *Making it Work for You* section at the end of this chapter to move closer to the powerful/Queen side.

Finally, in thinking about locus of control be aware of how your view of yourself may differ from how you view others facing parallel challenges. A study by researchers Jones and Nisbett[5] found that when conflicts arise in *our own* lives, we are more likely to attribute them to environmental (external) issues, but when *other people* face similar crises, we attribute that to defects in their character (internal). In other words we often give ourselves environmental excuses while expecting more personal responsibility from others. This tendency to excuse ourselves and expect more from others is another example of the subtle but insidious ways external thinking can find its way into our minds.

Important Points to Remember

- There are times when it is best to give up, cut your losses and move in another direction. You cannot fight every battle. So if the goal is not that important to you or you really have done all you can do, then pat yourself on the back for your efforts, reflect on what you've learned, and simply move on.
- Despite the hackneyed and misleading clichés that we often are inundated with, not everything is possible. So be ambitious, but

stay within the world of reason. I have seen too many people beat themselves up unnecessarily because they "failed" at virtually unattainable goals.

- Instead of subscribing to the "everything happens for a reason" philosophy, try *creating* your own positive meaning for whatever does happen. That will take you much further.

Persistence and Challenging Einstein

Persistence…The word alone is enough to bring a chorus of groans from even the most sincere acolytes of resilience among us. This reality notwithstanding, persistence is as valuable as it is frustrating.

What is it exactly? For our purposes persistence can be defined as continually expending effort, even when the target of that effort does not appear to have been impacted.

It's not that resilient people don't experience the frustration associated with persistence—they simply continue anyway. Their willingness and ability to engage in this unpleasant task cannot be extricated from our previous discussions on meaning and locus of control. Extended persistence is only possible when the target of our efforts is important to us and we simultaneously believe deeply that our actions will in fact impact that target in our desired fashion.

At the risk of appearing hypocritical, I am going to introduce a surprising addition to our list of prerequisites for resilience: *faith*. Bear with me here. When I speak of faith, I am not speaking of its close cousin destiny. Destiny implies that things will turn out a certain way regardless of our activity or inactivity. This is a hallmark of external locus of control thinking and not descriptive of resilient approaches to challenges at all. Faith in our context is different. Resilient people have faith but not faith in destiny. Instead they put most of their faith in a single overriding idea:

in our universe effort eventually gets rewarded. If one can hold dearly to that belief, even when it doesn't *appear* valid, then persistence can be sustained.

This is the good news about persistence. While it can often be maddeningly exasperating, it doesn't have to be. In studying resilient people, it became clear that many of them are able to be persistent because they have learned to remove much of the angst from the process. And the primary way they do this is by making *process* paramount.

How? While I'd like to take credit for the following observation about our physical world, someone narrowly beat me to it...by about three hundred years. In 1687 Sir Isaac Newton presented his laws of motion in his somnolently titled *Philosophie Naturalis Principia Mathematic.* In it his third law is the famous "For every action, there is an equal and opposite reaction." What's the connection to persistence and making *process paramount?* Resilient people operate under the assumption that each action they take in support of their objectives, no matter how seemingly inconsequential or ineffectual, *must* bear fruit to some extent. Why? Because Newton said so. He basically said that if you put *it* out there (whatever *it* is) there *must* be an equivalent and corresponding effect. Effort has impact, it's the law.

Case in point. At the moment I am typing these very words it is Thursday, November 1, 2012 at approximately 7:38 p.m. I live on the Jersey Shore, and Hurricane Sandy hit four days ago. My family and I (seven in total, including in-laws and nieces) are at a friend's small apartment twenty-five minutes away from home, taking turns with our first hot showers since the storm. My sister-in-law and mother-in-law had three and a half feet of water in their houses, and we all lost electricity. We have spent the last three days cleaning up waterlogged everything, and all of our bones are cold and achy.

So, why do I take out my laptop and write? Because I am practicing persistence. No matter how bad things are now, I know that if I keep "doing," it will eventually be rewarded. So we keep cleaning, and I keep writing. I have faith that eventually things will get cleaned up, and eventually these words will find your eyes. I can't know this for sure, but what I do know is that all the efforts will pay off in one way or another, no matter the context.

A key phrase of the preceding sentence however is "one way or another." The guarantee is not that things will always turn out the way you intend. The guarantee is that the action will have *an* impact. What exactly that impact will be we cannot know for certain. But generally speaking, if the actions are strategic and focused they *should,* eventually, achieve their intended results. It is the likelihood of these outcomes that sustains the process of persistence.

One of the greatest impediments to engaging in persistent behavior is that at first glance it can appear counterintuitive. In order to do it, you must challenge arguably the greatest genius of the twentieth century, Albert Einstein.

You may be aware of Einstein's famous definition of insanity: "doing the same thing over and over again and expecting different results." Well, get your straightjackets ready because in order to be persistent, we must defy him and do the same thing over and over again (perhaps adjusting our approach if necessary) *until* we get different results. Essentially, that is what persistence is—knocking on one hundred doors until one finally opens. Most people cannot take that sort of chronic disappointment and the resulting frustration, and they eventually give up. Why do resilient people keep knocking? Two simple reasons—they believe that eventually a door will open, and they really want what's inside.

To gain a better understanding of what is meant by persistence within a resilience context, we are going to reacquaint ourselves with someone who, despite recent feature films about him, we probably don't know as well as we thought—Abraham Lincoln. No, he was not a vampire hunter. But he was incredibly persistent.

For those of you who slept through US History, here are some of the setbacks Honest Abe had to contend with on his way to Mount Rushmore: Lincoln was born on February 12, 1809…yes, in a log cabin, in Hardin County, Kentucky. In 1812 his little brother died. In 1816 his family lost their house and land to debt. When he was nine years old his mother died from poisoned milk. In 1832 he wanted to go to law school but couldn't get in. In 1833 his business failed. In 1835 his fiancé died mysteriously. In 1836 he had a nervous breakdown. In 1838 he lost his election for speaker of the house. In 1843 he was defeated in his nomination for congress. In 1849 he sought the job of land officer in his home state but was rejected. In 1854 he lost his senate election. In 1856 he lost in his election for vice-president. In 1858 he lost his second nomination for senate.

Finally, in 1860 he was elected sixteenth president of the United States.

I don't know about you, but just reading his story makes me want to curl up in the fetal position and suck my thumb.

So what made Lincoln persist? Simple. There were things he really wanted to do, and he believed he could do them.

Accepting and Expecting Obstacles: *The Remarkable power of an* **If/Then Mindset**

Are obstacles along a path really obstacles if they were expected all along? While you mull that over, let's think about how resilient people begin their climbs out of whatever holes they find themselves in. They often do this by either consciously or unconsciously developing an "if/then" mentality visa vie potential impediments, and they do so at the very beginning of their journeys. An if/then mentality means starting the voyage *knowing* that problems will occur, and thinking *ahead of time* about pertinent strategies and responses- *If* I don't get the loan from the bank, *then* I may have to take out a second mortgage.…. *If* the United States does not have an effective treatment, *then* I will look to Canada.…*If* the judge gives me ten years, *then* I will plan my escape from custody, etc.

Resilient people go into the fire knowing they will probably get burned, and thinking of ways to minimize or avoid the effects. Consequently, these know "barriers" cease to be barriers. If I have an 8AM meeting with my boss, and I accept and expect there will be traffic/delays along the way, is that traffic a barrier to my getting there on time? Not really. While I may not know exactly where the traffic will be, I begin my drive *expecting* there will be delays. So in addition to leaving earlier, I plan some alternative routes: *If* the express lane of the Garden State Parkway is backed up, then I will switch to the local at the service area; *If* there is an accident on the NJ Turnpike, *then* I will use Route 9 instead; *If* the side streets near campus are congested, *then* I will drive on the sidewalk.

The if/then mindset is not just about strategy (though it is effective in this way), more importantly it is about *the relationship between the individual and adversity.* That relationship should be one of expectation and respect, but not of awe or subservience. Emerging challenges and difficulties are not separate entities to be dreaded, nor are they all-powerful beings to be infused with mystical power over us. They are simply hurdles; some we can go over, some under, and some we can simply lift and toss to the side. The repeated practice of this expected/accepted relationship with adversity creates in us a habit of looking at our paths of resilience as a series of situations to be managed, rather than as overwhelming evils to be feared and from which we must cower.

The nature of our relationship with adversity correlates closely with our previous discussions on self-efficacy and locus of control. *Expecting* adversity and responding to it bolsters our sense of personal agency - the challenges are there, but with work and skill we can move beyond them.

Conversely, if the challenges are viewed as pessimistic messages from the universe or simply "beyond us," we have little chance to do anything about them. We must simply cross our metaphorical fingers and hope they take mercy on us.

A visit with a recently divorced woman desperately trying to avoid growing old alone can help us see the significant benefits of applying an if/then mentality to our resilient journeys.

Janice divorced her husband after 12 years of thoroughly unhappy marriage. Six months had passed since the actually divorce decree was finalized, and one thing she'd learned about herself for certain was that while she was terrified of the idea of dating again, she was even more terrified of growing old alone. She could not seem to escape a dreaded image: herself, grey and wrinkled, surrounded by a brood of mangy felines.

With some help from a friend, Janice applied an if/then mentality while creating a detailed plan to find a new life partner, one who would actually last a lifetime.

While she would have loved to have the first man she dated be The One, she knew this would be unlikely. Consequently, she accepted that failure, perhaps lots of it, would precede success and planned accordingly. In addition to strategizing how to meet quality men, she was determined to learn from her mistake and not settle for someone with whom she was not completely compatible. After some deep soul searching she knew she'd rather be alone than unfulfilled, or perhaps even worse, twice divorced. She promised herself she'd resist the temptation to trade security for love.

Her first method for meeting men was to have friends set up her up. This yielded five dates, each one more disastrous than the previous. This initial pool included one 44 year old who not only lived at home but still had *Star Wars* sheets on his twin bed; a 35 year old who had no idea who the Beatles were; and a handsome architect who, the morning after their date, decided to reconcile with his wife. The idea that perhaps she wasn't *meant* to be in a fulfilling relationship crept into her mind, but after reminding herself that this was *supposed* to be difficult, she was emboldened to keep on keeping on.

So even with her confidence and ego on life support, she moved to plan B. Now that her initial strategy of being set up by friends had not yielded any fruit, she would try online dating.

Like clothes shopping at a thrift shop, the internet produced significantly more quantity than quality. Most of the potential mates' profile photos sported outdated clothing and hairstyles representative of the late 1980s and early 1990s, consequently when she actually met them they were significantly balder and fatter than she'd been led to believe. The misrepresentation went beyond the photos, carrying into career, education and sometimes even relationship status. Four dates in to the experiment, visions of her future self returned- elderly and encircled by cats. But once again, she returned to the plan and noted that if online dating did not work, she was supposed to join at least three clubs or organizations based on activities she enjoyed.

Several months later she met Wendell, also a new member of the hiking club she'd joined. He too was divorced and looking for a long term committed relationship. The two dated for six months, at which point he proposed. And while she liked Wendell a great deal, she really did, she did not love him. When she started her journey she promised herself she would not settle, and did so because she knew she might be tempted. So recalling that the plan was- *if the man is nice but that she did not love him, then she was to continue looking*- she let Wendell down with as much compassion and kindness as possible. While it was difficult to forgo the comfort and security of Wendell, the fact that she'd foreseen this very possibility made doing the right thing that much easier.

Several months later she met Maurice at a Latin dance class she'd taken, and knew instantly she'd done the right thing with Wendell. Janice and Maurice eventually moved in together, and remain in a committed relationship. Recently, the two went to the local pet store and brought home a large black Labrador Retriever.

Janice began her journey *knowing* there was a strong possibility of short-term failure, and planned alternatives. By adopting this if/then mentality, potentially devastating road closures became manageable detours.

Delaying Gratification

We are an "I need it now!" society. No doubt about it. We complain if the pizza takes more than half an hour to be brought to our home (and it must be hot). Thanks to ATMs we rarely stand in line at the bank. We demand information now (newspapers be damned, they are way too slow!). And we grow impatient if the car in front of us is not going *faster* than the speed limit. Even e-mail is being relegated to the slow lane and losing out to texts, Tweets, and Instagram. In twenty-first-century America, yesterday is too late.

Perhaps the most telling evidence of our impatience is the fact that the average American credit card debt per borrower is about five thousand dollars and is on the rise, having increased by 4.9 percent in the third quarter of 2012[6] (Translation: these folks wanted stuff they couldn't afford and lacked the patience to wait for it). And in what is probably the grandest example of the inability to delay gratification in all of human history, the United States currently has a national debt of *over* $16,000,000,000,000! (that is 16 trillion for those of us who haven't taken a math class in a while).

So what does this all mean in the context of resilience? A lot.

As we've discussed, when talking about recovering from trauma, we are usually talking about relatively severe ordeals—our focus here is not on people who are managing to overcome hangnails and paper cuts. And while the severity of the traumas to which we are referring can vary greatly, by definition they are not easily and quickly resolved. Therefore, virtually all resilience processes take lots of time and include multiple setbacks. This is why resilience is often referred to as a journey, sometimes an expedition, but never a "weekend jaunt." The long and obstructed road of resilience requires not only the ability to believe in the impact of our efforts but the ability to wait patiently for those efforts to bear fruit. In other words, *delaying gratification.*

Delaying gratification refers to committing actions (or enduring hardships) in the present while accepting the fact that the payoff is off in the future somewhere, and sometimes the *distant* future at that. However, the ubiquitous expectation that we can all have whatever we want right now—evidenced in part by the extensive credit card debt—makes working and waiting for what we want almost unbearable. The problem is we often refuse to be patient, even when we *know*, beyond the shadow of a doubt, that it's the best thing to do.

I have posed the following question (though I have changed the amounts given now that it is being targeted to adults) to literally hundreds of high school and college students and their responses are always telling. Before I contaminate your answer with my thoughts, try answering the following question as *honestly* as you can:

I give you a choice of two options.

- Option 1: I give you five thousand dollars cash right now.
- Option 2: I give you a certified check (that you know is good and can be taken to any bank) for ten thousand dollars, but you must wait nine months before you cash it.

Which option do you choose?

If you chose option one, don't worry. While you're not alone, you have revealed some impatience and difficulty with delaying gratification.

Ask any financial expert and she'll tell you that unless you're about to be homeless or owe the mob money, taking the five thousand dollars is not the wise choice. With the ten thousand dollars you are guaranteed to double your money simply by waiting, but many refuse to do so.

If you chose option two, congratulations. You are well on your way to understanding the value of patiently working now (or enduring a lack of something) for what you want later.

One of the ways I convince high school and college students of the overwhelming benefits of delaying gratification is by using the example of graduating from college.

I call it "The Million Dollar Decision."

Going to college is the ultimate exercise in delaying gratification. The underlining belief system of college attendance is that if I work hard now (and spend four or five years in college), I will have a better career later. Think about the financial investment you are really making with your choice to go to college; not only is the time you spend in college time you're not working and making money, but you actually pay (a lot!) for the privilege of attendance. So it is a financial double whammy (earnings lost plus expenses paid). On the surface it looks like a really bad investment. So why do so many people do it? Because in the long run it pays off, big time.

Here is where that million dollars comes in. According to the US Department of Commerce and Bureau of the Census,[7] if you drop out of high school to go to work, you'll earn on average about $27, 650 a year. If you delay gratification and finish high school, it jumps to $37,030. And if you complete your four-year degree (more gratification delay), $60,910. And remember, that is each year. If we take the difference between the high school completion salary and the college completion salary ($60,910–$37,030), we get $23,880 *per year!* Note that the average person will work about forty-five years after college. That means that over the course of their working lives, those who complete their college degree will make on average $1,074,600 *more* than those who dropped out. And remember, that's if you do finish high school. If you don't that number jumps to 1.5 million. Now that is a Million Dollar Decision!

The benefits of being able to delay gratification go beyond monetary. Research has correlated propensity to control impulse with a variety of quality of life indicators.

In undoubtedly the most famous study of its kind, often referred to as "The Marshmallow Study," Walter Mischel of Stanford University[8] placed four-year-old children in front of a plate with a marshmallow on it and told them that he would soon leave the room, and if they were patient enough to wait until his return they would get *two* marshmallows, but if not, then only the one. Most of the children (about two-thirds) were indeed able to wait until the researcher's return (exhibiting impulse control and the ability to delay gratification) and the others were not.

Even for those who were able to wait, the task was not easy. These children employed a variety of techniques to help the time go faster and to distract themselves from the treat in front of them. Some covered their eyes, some tapped their feet, and some even tried to go to sleep. (Want some fun? Go to YouTube and search "Marshmallow test" and watch kids struggle with impulse control!)

This research was initially conducted in the 1960s, thus the researchers were able to take a longitudinal view of the children to see if and how their early dispositions toward delayed gratification may have impacted their lives. The differences among the "waiters" and the "grabbers" were striking. According to researchers the waiters were more socially adept, more likely to accept challenges, more persistent, more self-reliant, and more goal-directed. Those who were unable to wait were less adept in these areas and appeared less decisive and more easily frustrated, and they exhibited shorter tempers. The differences between the groups went beyond these somewhat abstract and subjective personality traits.

The waiters scored 210 points higher on their combined SAT scores as compared to the grabbers.

The fact that it was difficult for even the waiters to wait speaks to the inherent challenge of delaying gratification. Expending energy in the present for a payoff that may be months or years away is not something that comes easily to us Homo sapiens. Back when we were in the wild, simply trying to survive on a daily basis, most of our energies had to be targeted in the present. There were too many immediate potentially lethal threats to consider. However, with civilization came relative safety, comfort, and predictability. In this new world, planning and waiting have become imperatives.

However difficult it may be, almost without exception resilient people possess this ability to work now for what they want later. Consequently, a logical next question would be can impulse control and delaying gratification be taught? The answer appears to be yes, but that it is difficult to do so. Evidence as to the difficulty of teaching delayed gratification can be found in the fact that variations in ability appear at very young ages (e.g., the four-year-olds in the study). This finding leads to the belief that genetic and physiological differences are at play. However, while some of us may be *predisposed* to being more or less impulsive, there is no doubt that individuals can improve their ability to control impulse and delay gratification—it's called maturity.

As we mature and gain life experience, we are better able to think long-term and connect past actions with present outcomes. But as anybody with adolescent children will tell you, trying to rush or force maturity is like trying to coerce the clouds to give you rain. You can threaten or bribe them as much as you like, but they won't release their moisture until they are good and ready. You cannot compel maturity; you can only set the stage.

Going back to the marshmallow study, think for a moment how relatively easy it would be for you as an adult to wait five minutes for twice as much of whatever you want. For example, if I said, "Here is one hundred dollars. You can take it and leave, or you can hang out here for five minutes, and I'll give you two hundred dollars." What would you do? Unless you had a *serious*, like clinical, case of *I need it right now!*, you would wait without breaking a sweat. However, extend five minutes to six months, and you may be out the door and on your way to the mall. So while we all get better at increasing our ability to delay gratification as we get older, because the stakes and time periods also expand, we may still struggle.

Like anything else, before we can address it in ourselves we should see what "it" really is for us. Below is another survey and can help shed some light on where we stand vis-à-vis this significant attribute.

Delayed Gratification Self-Survey

Think about your life and your own ability (or inability) to be patient and delay gratification. Take the following brief quiz. Put a "1" if the statement does not describe you, a "2" if the statement describes you somewhat, and a "3" if it is highly descriptive

(1=not descriptive, 2=somewhat descriptive, 3=highly descriptive).

*Again, be honest! This is not about getting "right" answers—it's about self-discovery.

----

1. When I get money, I spend it immediately on whatever I want at the time. _____
2. I don't mind waiting a long time at a restaurant as long as the food is good. _____
3. I often settle for things that I don't really want because I am too impatient. _____
4. Generally speaking I would describe myself as a patient person. _____
5. I find it difficult to plan ahead more than a day or two. _____

6. When I start a diet or a workout regime, I am good at sticking with it. _____

7. When I set long-range goals, I tend to quit before I reach them. _____

8. I am uncomfortable buying things that I am not certain that I can afford. _____

9. I find it difficult to sacrifice now in order to benefit my future. _____

10. I think it is important to plan for the future as much as you can. _____

11. I will do almost anything to feel comfortable in the present moment, even if I know it's not good for me in the long run. _____

12. Planning is one of my best qualities. _____

13. I don't really have faith that what I do will make much of a difference in the long run._____

14. When it comes to money, I would describe myself as a "saver." _____

15. I think people should live for today and not worry much about planning for tomorrow._____

16. I try to eat healthy food as much as possible so I can live a long life. _____

17. If I won the lottery tomorrow, I'd rather get one hundred thousand dollars immediately rather than fifty thousand dollars per year for three years. _____

18. I'm usually able to sacrifice for a future goal. _____

19. I use (or would use) my credit card to purchase items now that I can't yet afford. _____

20. I'm good at saving up for stuff I really want. _____

Scoring:

A. Add up your scores for the odd numbered statements and put your total here: _____

B. Add up your scores for the even numbered statements and put your total here: _____

C. Now find the difference between the two numbers: _____

D. Now check "DGW" if your odd score is higher and check "DGS" if your even score is higher. DGW _____ or DGS _____

E. (Final Score) Your answer to letter C _____ and check your response to letter D: DGW_____ or DGS_____

DGW = Delayed Gratification Weak

DGS = Delayed Gratification Strong

DGW 20---------------10-------------0---------------10-----------20 DGS

Impatient---Patient

Where are you on the scale? Are you happy with your score? In the "Making it Work for You" section we will review a plan to improve our ability to delay gratification.

Making it Work for You

Manifesting an Internal Locus of Control

Here is a five-step activity plan that you can begin right now to maximize your internal locus of control.

1. Identify some important goals that you have (remember, "important" means important to YOU, not others).

2. Make a list of ten actions you could take right now, this week, or over the next two weeks that will bring you closer to those goals.

3. Once you have completed each action, place a check next to it.

4. After every five checks, provide yourself with a reward (e.g., a night out, a nap, a movie, etc.).

5. As you continue updating and editing your list every two weeks, pay extra attention to the connection between your *actions* and the *desired outcomes*. Awareness of these causes and effects (i.e., "performance accomplishments") will bolster your internal locus

of control and hopefully provide you with the energy you need. When/if you do get a bit discouraged or lazy, concentrate on those specific instances where action has had positive results. That evidence should help drive you to action. Finally, if you are being active and not seeing results, you may be doing things that are not in line with your goals. Try different actions until results appear.

If you cannot bolster your self-efficacy through focus on past achievements, try some of the

other sources discussed earlier using the prompts below.

Vicarious Experience: Read about or talk with other people who have successfully dealt with a challenge or obstacle similar to the one you presently face. Think about how what they did made a difference and how you can emulate them. Remember, if it worked for them it can work for you.

Verbal Persuasion: Seek out supportive people whom you trust, respect, and admire. Heed their wisdom and advice as motivation to act and persist.

Physiological States: Monitor and scrutinize your emotions and mood and how they may be impeding your belief in yourself and your agency. Practice manipulating your emotional status and placing yourself in physiological states that promote optimism and self-confidence.

Finally, as we will see in the chapter on "returning to the spring," social interactions and intimate relationships can actually increase our confidence levels and bolster our self-efficacy. Consequently, you may want to engage in the above activities with a friend and/or simply share your goals and objectives with those in your life that love and support you. The power of pulling others along on our resilience journeys cannot be underestimated.

Whether it is through one activity or an amalgamation, if you can manage to increase your degree of self-efficacy, even a little, the potential payoff can be enormous.

Persistence 101

Persistence can be enhanced by (1) believing wholeheartedly in the impact of your actions and (2) focusing more on process than outcome. In addition to these overriding belief systems, I will share a specific approach that I have personally found very effective, particularly when the goal you are trying to achieve isn't overly complicated but is rather especially energy- and time-consuming.

I have adapted this approach from the work of time management pioneer Alan Lakein[9] and his "Swiss-Cheese" method. This can be a powerful visual metaphor and a simple reminder to keep us nibbling away at seemingly gargantuan tasks that take large amounts of time to complete. This approach to persistence works especially well when combined with the other two pillars of effective action: self-efficacy and delayed gratification. This is not a book on time management techniques, but for the sake of promoting any latent persistence genes we may have, let's take a brief detour.

When it comes to persistence, the tortoise is king; slow and steady win the race. The key is to utilize our time gradually and consistently so we keep making progress but don't run out of steam.

This is where the Swiss-Cheese approach comes in.

Think of all the tasks you must complete to bounce back from your trauma as a huge, flat piece of cheese. The focus is on putting as many holes in it as possible. The holes represent completion of significant tasks and the taking of steps toward your larger resilience goals. Instead of trying to do everything at once (e.g., pulling an all-nighter or making a risky broad-sweeping gesture) you poke small holes (complete smaller tasks) *consistently* and throughout the days and weeks.

The key here is consistency of action not size. *Success* magazine editor and author Darren Hardy coined a term for the surprising power of steady purposeful action and used it as a title for his book, *The Compound*

Effect.[10] As he points out over and over again, while it's not dramatic and exciting, it's an incredibly effective route to a substantial and sustainable accomplishment.

Even small amounts of time here and there can make a difference— just keep poking holes, no matter their size. Twenty minutes right when you wake up, another twenty after breakfast, twenty before lunch, twenty while waiting at the dentist's office, etc. After a while, if you are consistent and diligent enough, you'd be amazed at what you can achieve, all without burning yourself out. Granted, it's not very sexy, but it can be incredibly effective. The natural world is filled with illustrations of the benefits of the Swiss-Cheese method.

Have you ever been to the Grand Canyon? It's one of the most hyped tourist destinations in the world, yet, for me at least, its beauty and size did not disappoint. The Grand Canyon is truly awesome; the Colorado River runs through it for 277 miles, and it's over a mile deep at certain points. So what created it? Maybe a huge asteroid crash? Or a sudden and fierce earthquake? The answer is much less grand (pun intended) but more telling. The Grand Canyon was formed slowly by water and erosion over the course of hundreds of millions of years. Essentially, mother nature applied the Swiss-Cheese approach and created one of the seven natural wonders of the world. That must have been one hell of a hunk of cheese.

Energy Efficiency

All this talk of action and work is vital, but what is equally valuable is *where* we focus our energies. If you are doing the wrong stuff, it doesn't matter how many holes you punch in the cheese. You can turn that cheese into fine mesh and still won't get where you need to be. Hopefully, assuming you worked the acceptance and meaning steps effectively, your actions should be on target. But if you fear you may veer of course once in a while, the following could help you expend energy where you get the most bang for your buck.

While each situation and contest is unique, there is a proven method that can help maximize efficacy and efficiency by spending time on what matters. It's called the 80-20 rule. Like many of the concepts discussed, while many resilient individuals may have been unaware of the particulars, this has not stopped them from applying it regularly.

I love pithy truths. There is something so refreshing about compact and concise validity. The 80-20 rule (aka the "Pareto Principle) is one of my favorites. You may be familiar with this widely used rule of thumb; basically it says that in many contexts roughly 80 percent of effects come from 20 percent of causes. The principle is often used in marketing and sales, where, for example, 80 percent of the sales may come from the best 20 percent of sales people. Or in campaign fundraising, 80 percent of the funds that are raised come from 20 percent of donors. While this is not a scientifically proven ratio, I have observed it in action on multiple occasions and in a variety of contexts. For example, in most of my classes it seems that 20 percent of the students provide 80 percent of the discussion. In many of my work places, 20 percent of the people I associated with influenced 80 percent of what happened to me. If you go and look in your closets, you will probably find that you wear 20 percent of your clothes 80 percent of the time (I hope this doesn't apply to your socks and underwear, but you get the point). Finally, when reading nonfiction (except in this case) 80 percent of what is valuable will come from 20 percent of the book.

By turning this concept around a bit and using this 80-20 ratio as a guide for where to expend energy, you can efficiently focus on doing what needs to be done in order to climb out of whatever hole you may find yourself in.

Think about all of the stuff you need to do to overcome your challenge (all the potential holes in your cheese). Are all of them equally efficacious? Probably not. According to the Pareto Principle, 20 percent of them will provide you with 80 percent of what you need. As you are nibbling away and creating your Swiss-Cheese, try and spend as much of that time as possible on that 20 percent.

Despite late night infomercial claims, there is no substitute for massive and continuous action (read "work") if we want to bounce back from one of life's massive beat downs. Cultivating a strong sense of self-efficacy, being doggedly unrelenting, believing that the universe always rewards action, and being prepared to wait for those rewards are all keys. However, the catch-22 is that often it is the moment just after we've been beaten down that we are most drained of the energies that we so desperately need to get back up. This makes the expulsion of energy and the committing of action the last things we want to do. Consequently, the question becomes, how do we put ourselves in the right frame of mind and state of physiological readiness so that we have the energy to climb up the ladder when necessary? Answer: We must return to our spring.

CHAPTER 5:
RETURNING TO THE SPRING:
IDENTIFYING, USING, AND
VALUING OUR PERSONAL
CHARGING STATIONS

"I wonder what's on TV tonight?"

When was the last time you stayed up all night? If you're over thirty, I'd bet it was a while ago, but try and remember how you felt physically. And that was only one night! What if you had to give up sleep for a week? Or even half that? *If* you survived, I'm sure it wouldn't be pretty. But *why* exactly?

Virtually all animals sleep, and while scientists don't fully understand this ubiquitous need, obviously the overriding purposes are physical and emotional rest and replenishment. We all know how irritable, ineffective, lethargic, and downright pissy we can get without enough sleep, but there is a related type of replenishment that gets far less attention: the replenishing of our overall "life force levels" (for lack of a better term).

This chapter gets at specific ways that resilient people *maintain* their minds, bodies, spirits, and souls before, during, and after crises hit. Think of the prior Action phase as auto mechanics repairing your car after a major collision, but think of this recharging concept as ongoing maintenance (e.g., oil changes, checking fluids, etc.) that keeps your car running as smoothly as possible, and in the best shape possible to withstand and recover from the accidents or breakdowns that may be waiting around every literal and figurative corner. Acceptance, Meaning, and Action are the driving components of resilience, but making certain you can execute them effectively is equally vital, and that's where our charging stations come in.

If we are required to stretch ourselves in the process of living resilience, then we must make certain that we are physically, mentally, emotionally, and spiritually primed. To return to our rubber metaphor, we must make certain our personal consistency is as sturdy and durable as possible while maintaining a degree of flexibility. Simply put, the objective is to manufacture heavy-duty rubber. Resilient people understand this on some level, and as a result have built-in mechanisms for keeping themselves limber and prepared, "raring to go."

The manifestations of these charging stations vary from person to person; they can be places, activities, rituals, sacred texts or even people. But what they all have in common is that on a regular basis they provide the physiological, emotional, intellectual, and/ or spiritual replenishment and respites necessary for stressed individuals to then rejoin the fray. Resilient people identify, cultivate, nurture, value, and utilize their charging stations consistently so that life force levels are optimized.

The existence and value of this life force notion is not a new idea and nor is it unique to resilience studies. Asian traditions refer to it as our "chi," or "qigong." Judeo-Christian traditions may refer to it as our "spirit" or "soul," and perhaps most appropriately, Native American traditions refer to it as "the great mystery." Even pop culture has words for the concept. In the 1999 comedy *Austin Powers: The Spy Who Shagged Me,* the eponymous character struggles to regain his "mojo," and urban cultures often talk of getting your "groove" or "swag" back. Though they all seem to fall a bit short, these myriad terms are attempts to capture this nebulous but precious stuff.

The life of the famous singer/performer Tina Turner, particularly her use of a Japanese Buddhist tradition called Nichiren, is a well-known illustration of how a spiritual practice can facilitate substantial resilience.

Turner was born Anna Mae Bullock to Tennessee sharecroppers in 1939. Blessed with looks, talent, and an exceptional singing voice, she rose to fame as part of "The Ike and Tina Revue" with her eventual husband, Ike Turner.

They were stars and seemed to be living the American dream, but, as is often the case, the reality was much darker. Behind the scenes Ike Turner physically and emotionally abused Tina for over a decade. The physical abuse was so brutal, she eventually needed reconstructive surgery to fix the damage done to her face. In 1974 she finally garnered the courage to leave him, in large part due to having been introduced to the practice of Nichiren Buddhism and chanting by a friend.

Tina reported that when she left her abusive husband, literally running away from the hotel where they were staying at the time, all she had was the thirty-six cents in her pocket. Amazingly, during the divorce proceedings, all she asked for was to keep her stage name—*Tina Turner.* She believed in herself deeply and knew that eventually she would regain her stature and make it on her own. Through her subsequent solo performances, she climbed out of financial ruin and earned both monetary and critical acclaim, having won eight Grammy awards in the process. To this day she continues her spiritual practice and describes it as an essential key of her ongoing resilience.

Though not writing specifically about resilience, in Thomas Moore's renowned *Care of the Soul,*[1] the author captures the profound implications of nurturing (or neglecting) our deepest selves, and in the process helps us understand its crucial nature. Especially relevant to our discussion is Moore's introduction where he writes, "The great malady of the twentieth century, implicated in all of our troubles and affecting us individually and socially, is 'loss of soul.' When soul is neglected, it doesn't just go away; it appears symptomatically in obsessions, addictions, violence, and loss of meaning."

Knowing what we now know about what it takes to be resilient, it is difficult to overstate the relevance of self-replenishment and an ongoing nurturing of our own "great mysteries." Consequently, what follows is a detailed look at what these activities may look like, how they work, and a guide to help you find those most suitable for you.

Regardless of what words are used for the life forces we are referring to, most resilient people report that paying close attention to this illusive concept's care and replenishment is an indispensable part of their daily lives.

How and Why It Matters

The nexus between our regeneration of life force levels and our optimization of resilience behaviors necessitates a deeper understanding of how and why our physiology and cognition are so closely connected.

There is now a growing body of robust evidence documenting the mind-body connection and its effects on our overall quality of life.

Researchers refer to these connections and related outcomes as the *biopsychosocial* paradigm, an idea first formally articulated as a valid scientific concept as recently as 1977 by a psychiatrist named George Engel.[2] Engel was fascinated with psychosomatic incidents he had been observing and helped create biopsychosocial phenomena as a field of study.

Though it pains me to reflect upon it, as a child I had a severe case of that dreaded disease "Sundaynightitis" (Unfortunately, I think I passed it on to my own kids). Sundaynightitis is characterized by sudden and intense tummy aches, which, as the name implies, bizarrely only strike on Sunday evenings. (It seems that Sundaynightitis afflicts millions of children nationwide, and the only known cure appears to be three-day weekends and summer vacation!) What was interesting about my particular case of Sundaynightitis was that often after simply *thinking* about having to go to school the next morning, I *truly began to feel sick*. You see, in a way, I wasn't faking. I did start feeling sick on Sunday nights beginning at whatever time the sun went down and we could no longer play outside. Now, we could have a long philosophical conversation about whether or not my tummy aches were "real," but what I know for certain is they felt real. And to a sick person, isn't that all that really matters? While I could not have articulated it at the time, this experience was my first exposure to the mind-body connection.

The *placebo effect* is among the earliest and most evaluated evidence for the direct connection between what we think and how we feel. The placebo effect refers to the measurable efficacy of a therapy (usually a "medication") that contains no active therapeutic agents. In other words simply the act of doing (or taking) something that is *supposed* to help can actually help. (In a sense this is what my father experienced as a child. He was "all better" when the doctor told him he should be.)

How often do placebos work? Most research indicates that, at least initially, placebos work between 30 percent and 40 percent of the time.

This provides more evidence that how we feel physically is inextricably enmeshed with our thoughts, beliefs, and emotions.

In a recent study conducted by Harvard University Medical School faculty member and director of the Program in Placebo Studies, Dr. Ted Kaptchuk,[3] 59 percent of patients taking a placebo to relieve symptoms of their irritable bowel syndrome reported their symptoms had been alleviated adequately, compared to only 35 percent of those in the control group. Given what we now know about placebos, this should not be a shock. However, what was a surprise was that in this case those taking the placebos *knew* they were placebos, and yet they *still* worked. This finding adds to both the mystery and possibilities of the mind-body connection.

While placebo studies provide valuable evidence by isolating specific variables and linking them to isolated outcomes, the types of regenerative charging reported by resilient individuals is more comprehensive in nature. That is, there appear to be a constellation of important characteristics that go into creating deeply rewarding restorative experiences.

Many resilient individuals describe the time they spend engaging in these recharging activities as essentially creating necessary metaphysical and emotional distance from a daily challenge or pressing crisis; it's a way of transcending the problem or daily trials, if only temporarily. These are much needed psycho-emotional respites from our daily grind worlds; they are essentially forms of *mental vacation.*

A common characteristic of these replenishment activities is they are often characteristic of what social scientists refer to as "flow." Flow occurs when we lose ourselves and our sense of time in the process of an activity; we are so fully engaged, immersed, and committed, that we almost "become one" with it. In his national best seller, *Flow: The Psychology of Optimal Experience,*[4] Mihaly Csikszentmihalyi describes "flow" as "joy, creativity, [and] the process of total involvement with life." He then goes on to describe how getting into flow not only accentuates our happiness but contributes significantly to our overall sense of well-being.

Flow often happens to artists when they paint, sculptors when their hands seem to move on their own, and writers when the words just keep flowing (or so I am told!). For many resilient people, flow comes from physical activities. For example, basketball players talk of getting in the "zone" where they no longer have to think when hitting shots and passing the ball, and runners talk about a "runners high" where they may experience intense euphoria followed by a quiet calm.

I had a student who recently ran (and finished) the twenty-six-mile New York City Marathon at the age of forty-seven. When I asked him how difficult the last ten miles were, he surprised me by saying, "Easy… it was the first ten that were the hardest." Once he got to the last ten, he was flowing.

Examples of Charging Station Phenomena

This charging station phenomenon can take many forms, some expected and some unusual, but if they accomplish the goals of providence, transcendence, and increased energy, then they are inherently valuable. Below, in no particular order, are some common examples and how they can play out. I then provide a list of additional activities as well as ideas on how you can identify and cultivate your own.

Prayer and Ecclesiastical Activities

Prayer and ecclesiastical activities are probably the most common vessels for life force regeneration in our society. And, as we've learned, the faithful among us are usually able to extract more meaning from life, thus bolstering our overall energy levels. Clearly there are distinct benefits from prayer and church/temple/mosque involvement, especially when people are in crisis. There is a reason that, according to a poll from the *Pew Research Center's Forum on Religion & Public Life*,[5] while about 32 percent of the American population describes themselves as "nonreligious," that number drops to 10 percent for those in prison. (Note: If we look at the number of prisoners who are full *atheists*, according to a 1997 *Federal Bureau of Prisons* report,[6] the percentage drops to less than 1 percent!) Apparently prison and the inherent hardships within can make believers out of almost all of us.

Research indicates that there is a good deal of validity to the idea that religion can serve as an effective mental-health tool (whether or not this is because of divine intervention or a placebo type effect is a question best saved for another forum). In his thorough review of hundreds of research articles on the topic, Dr. Harold Koenig of Duke University[7] came to some intriguing conclusions supporting the link between religion and physical/emotional health. The following were among the conclusions: The average hospital stay for churchgoers is three times shorter than for nonchurchgoers. Heart patients were over ten times more likely to survive after surgery if they practiced a religion. And religious people tend to suffer from depression less frequently than the nonreligious (and recover more quickly if they do succumb).

The act of prayer itself, usually defined as a reverent petition made to a god or a godlike entity, is common to most established religions. However, it should be noted that theoretically people can and do pray to and for almost anything (I have a friend who prays in vain to the baseball gods every spring for the New York Mets to win).

In addressing the much ballyhooed question of "Does prayer work?" we must first define what *working* means. If working means the instillation of a sense of restored vitality, meaningfulness, connectedness, and energy, then clearly prayer works for many people.

For religious prayers the act and routine of prayer itself often results in an inspired state which fortifies their overall spirit and outlook. Perhaps the most well-known ritualized prayer activity is the Islamic prayer system known as *Salat* (Arabic word for "prayer"). Salat is one of the five Pillars of Islam—these are the duties of every practicing Muslim. The others being testimony of faith (the declaration that Allah is the one and only god); giving (or *Zakat*), which emphasizes providing for the needy; fasting during the Ramadan; and the pilgrimage to Makkah (previously known as "Mecca").

Faithful practitioners of Islam must pray five times per day and face Makkah while doing so. The process is comprehensive and includes a good deal of physical activity (repetitive bending, kneeling, and bowing), oral elements (reciting verses from the *Qur'an*), and mental focus (the prayer may even be perceived as invalid without a *mindful* observance of Allah). For many practitioners, the process reinvigorates and bolsters overall energy levels, creating a sense of optimism.

I have the privilege of teaching in one of the most ethnically diverse universities in the world. As a result I have students from a variety of religious backgrounds and traditions. Several of my Islamic students have described the emotional boosts they get from their daily prayers and how the consistency and practice of the rituals have helped them endure often difficult lives as practicing Muslims in post-9/11 America. Omar's story below is an example.

Omar is a twenty-three-year-old college junior who, despite being an excellent student, has been taking longer than usual to earn his degree. He described the challenges he faces and the psychosocial benefits of Islamic prayer in the following way:

> I am a pretty happy guy all around, but I do feel beaten down sometimes. I mean it's hard for me sometimes because I feel

like I have to do everything...My parents moved here like fifteen years ago, but they still don't speak English well, so I have to be the translator, the negotiator and stuff, with the electric company, the gas company, with the immigration people all that...We don't have much money, so everything is a struggle. I mean, look at me. I'm twenty-three and still only technically a junior, barely. That's because I keep stopping and starting because if I don't have tuition or if I have to work more, then I just take less classes. Or sometimes if I have to take on more hours at work, then I just won't go to school that semester...Sometimes I get a bunch of shit from people I don't even know, making comments about terrorism or looking at me like I'm a criminal or whatever, and don't even get me started on airports...for spring break I was taking a bus to visit my cousins in Michigan, and we were all lined up to get on, and they just let everyone put their bags in that compartment below, but of course they inspected mine. They went through it and everything. It was so embarrassing...the guy went through all my stuff by hand; he even pulled out my underwear in front of everyone. I was so pissed, but what could I do? If I start complaining, who knows what they'd do... But I keep going and get up in the morning and do what I have to, and a big part is that I am committed to Islam and doing what I need to do. Each day can be a struggle, but I know that when I do my prayers, I'll get that lift I need to keep moving forward. No matter where I'm at or what I am doing, I'll stop and do my prayers, and almost every time I feel better afterward. The entire process is like a break from the world, like time to catch my breath. After, I know it will all be worth it, and life isn't so hard.

Omar's journey is a tough one. In addition to chronic financial pressures and the traditional hardships of being a recent immigrant, he has the added stress of being perceived as threatening and thus is treated with open hostility on a regular basis. These pressures would be enough to derail most people. He stays committed however, in large part because of his daily prayer activities and their restorative effects.

While each individual's relationship with prayer and religion is unique, there appear to be a good deal of crossover and shared opportunities for life-affirming benefits.

Mindfulness Meditation

What is mindfulness meditation? In the Buddhist tradition, mindfulness is one of the seven factors of enlightenment. The others are keen investigation of the *dhamma* (Buddhist scripture), energy, rapture or happiness, calm, concentration, and equanimity. The act of meditation itself is often characterized as a means to acquiring these factors. Mindfulness emphasizes awareness of the present moment and discourages judgment and ego (and based on our previous discussion we know what a potential toxin that can be). The physical act of meditation usually involves sitting quietly, concentrating on one's breathing, and focusing on the present moment. If and when anxieties and thoughts of past and future enter one's mind, one simply acknowledges them and returns to focusing on breathing and the present moment.

While this may sound easy, anyone who has ever tried it knows how surprisingly difficult and frustrating it can be. (While Buddhist monks can often meditate for hours on end, I think the longest I've ever gone has been about three and a half minutes.) But for millions of people around the world, the benefits are well worth it.

Empirical research has vigorously supported the efficacy of this ancient form of relaxation, and modern technology is now shedding light on the "hows" and "whys." Dr. Jon Kabat-Zinn[8] of the University of Massachusetts Medical School is among the most well-known experts on meditation and mental health. In a recent study, he and his colleagues split a group of forty-one highly stressed business people into two groups. One was taught to meditate and practiced it for eight weeks, and the other did not.

All of the study participants had their brainwaves evaluated on three occasions—at the beginning of the study, after the eight weeks, and four months later. The brain scans revealed that meditators actually shifted their brain activity to different areas of the brain's cortex. For this group, brainwaves that began in the stress-prone right frontal cortex moved to the calmer left side. According to neurologists this shift mitigates the degrees of stress, anxiety, and even mild depression experienced by the individual. Additionally, for these individuals, there was less electro-neural activity in the area of the brain that processes fear, the amygdale. Finally, when comparing the groups, those who meditated reported being both more relaxed and happier.

Mom's Story

Previously I shared the story of my father's illness as a boy and the impact it had on my outlook on life. Also, as referred to earlier, unfortunately— fair or not— the potential for serious illness is everywhere. While one can be buffered to an extent by First World living conditions and good medical insurance, unlike reality competition shows, there is no immunity.

My father's serious illness occurred closer to the start of the twentieth century, while my mother's laid in wait until the turn of the twenty-first. Her story provides concrete illustration of specifically how habitual "recharging" practices can facilitate resilience, even amid some of our most dreaded and agonizing hardships.

In the year 2000, while my mother was living in San Diego, California, and I was in New Jersey (as I said, life is not always fair), she was diagnosed with breast cancer. According to the National Cancer Institute, breast is the most common form of cancer among women, but this interesting little factoid does little to ease anxiety when a loved one is afflicted. After the initial shock of the diagnosis, I made it a point to call her on a regular basis to see how she was doing. At the time "How are you doing?" seemed to me such a hollow and empty question, but that's all I had.

She underwent chemotherapy once a month for five months and radiation treatments *every day* for six weeks. However, virtually every time I posed my lame question, she responded with a variation of the same response: "Well, I am OK in this very moment, and this very moment is all we have."

Wow. Talk about courage and character. It is easy to emphasize staying in the moment and *smelling roses* when things are going well. That is ultimate money-where-your-mouth-is time. But to maintain that approach while you are literally sick and tired and fighting for your life? Impressive. Most of us would say "Screw the damn roses. I'm pissed!"

So how did she do it? Medical marijuana perhaps? Well, in a way, like a champion prizefighter, she had been training for this fight for decades, since the late 1970s to be exact. For over thirty years (before it was hip and cool) she religiously practiced her form of life force regeneration— mindfulness meditation. And while as a child I found it a bit curious and sometimes annoying to have to be silent for forty-five-minute periods once per day, I now see why.

As her meditation practice developed over the decades, not only did it increase and improve her physical energy levels, it simultaneously relaxed her and increased her mental clarity. Surviving cancer *may* have been possible without her meditation practice; however, I'm certain that *thriving* postcancer would not. She has been cancer free for over a decade now and is more committed to her practice than ever.

When my mother began meditating all those years ago, obviously it was not to prepare specifically for a future cancer she could have had no way of knowing would come. However, her practice did provide her with a healthy outlook on life and kept her grounded and relatively stress free so when sickness came she'd be as ready as possible. This active maintenance of the soul and spirit facilitates our ability to practice resilience by keeping us in a state of perpetual psycho-physical-spiritual readiness.

Exposure to Nature

Groundbreaking Harvard developmental psychologist Howard Gardner,[9] whom we met earlier, challenged psychologists and educators to rethink some very basic questions about human potential and learning, most notably the question of what it really means to be "smart." Gardner originally theorized that there were seven distinct "intelligences." (Note: Gardner defines "intelligences" as "problem-solving and product-producing behaviors.") His initial list consisted of Visual/Spatial Intelligence, Logical/Mathematical Intelligence, Verbal /Linguistic Intelligence, Bodily/Kinesthetic Intelligence, Musical/Rhythmic Intelligence, Interpersonal Intelligence, Intrapersonal Intelligence, and Spatial/Visual Intelligence.

I really liked how his ideas prompted us to recast our views of what smart looks like, and I taught them in many of my classes to get future educators thinking about ways to vary how they teach and assess students—the main premise being that if learners are given an array of ways to show their smarts, then odds are more of them will be proficient.

Gardner never meant for his initial list to be exhaustive and later added a "new" intelligence, which he referred to as "Naturalistic." (Note: he subsequently also added a "Spiritual/Existential" Intelligence, as well as a "Moral" Intelligence.) Upon learning of his "Naturalistic" addendum, I initially thought, OK, here is where you lost me, Howard. The other seven I can understand, they are relatively cut and dry and more importantly can be measured empirically. But "Naturalistic," what the heck was that?

Essentially, when Gardner talks of a naturalistic intelligence, he is describing individuals who excel in and around natural and organic environments. These are people who not only appreciate the natural world and thrive in it, but who have a proclivity for understanding environmental ecosystems and are able to see the connectedness of all things.

I see the value of Gardner's take on naturalistic intelligence not so much in facilitating learning and assessment but rather in that he gets at the natural world's remarkable potency as a source of literal and figurative energy. For many people the natural world is an enormous Duracell battery. And given that, evolutionarily speaking, it was just yesterday that we all lived outside among and amid the trees, this makes a great deal of sense.

The potential of the natural world as a psycho-emotional resource can be evidenced in a multitude of ways. Many of us choose to hike, fish, swim, and camp on our vacations because we come back feeling refreshed in ways that staying home and watching television or going to Las Vegas simply cannot accomplish. Even simply sunbathing in Cancun is usually more restorative than playing video games or slot machines. And though it is not necessary to understand how nature does this in order to reap the benefits, there are chemical, physiological, and evolutionary reasons for these benefits.

My sister is a generally positive and upbeat person, but she knows each winter she is susceptible to melancholy if she does not get enough sun. So much so that she often uses all of her available vacation time in December through March, taking multiple trips to sunny locals near the equator. Though not clinically diagnosed, she is probably sad because of a mild case of SAD (Seasonal Affective Disorder). Luckily her case is minor and can be treated with frequent flyer miles.

Severe cases of SAD can cause anxiety, loss of energy, depression, hopelessness, and even social withdrawal. It only takes simple extrapolation to see that if lack of exposure to the sun can contribute to all of these negative outcomes, then ample exposure can facilitate their positive opposites. Unfortunately, many are falling into the former group and not the latter. Estimates of how many Americans suffer from SAD vary greatly, but the most common numbers cited appear to fall in the 10 to 20 percent range.

How can a simple case of limited exposure to sunlight cause such debilitating emotional impact? Actually, scientists and doctors are not completely certain. However, based on work done by the United Kingdom's National Health Service (NHS),[10] a leading theory is that lack of light negatively affects the hypothalamus. The hypothalamus is a part of the brain that, among other things, impacts our sleep patterns and emotions. The amount of light we take in through our eyes affects what our hypothalamus communicates to our body, thus influencing the production of both melatonin and serotonin, two hormones that help manage mood.

But again the science of *how* is less important than the reality of *what*. Many people achieve deep and profound senses of well-being and nourishment from extended time spent out of doors, and evolutionary scientists can tell us why.

As alluded to earlier, spending the majority of our time indoors is a relatively new cultural norm. Physiologically and evolutionarily speaking we are still built to be outside almost all of the time. Evidence of this predilection for natural surroundings can be found by digging deeper into in the physiology of our responses to light.

Did you know that even on an overcast day, the light outside is over ten times brighter than the average indoor light (and on a sunny day can be one hundred times greater than that!)? We possess light receptors in our brains that *only* respond to light levels that can be found outside. Natural light also plays a crucial role in the setting and running of our body clocks. It's no wonder that without enough *natural* light we can feel sluggish, imbalanced, and generally "off."

Exercise

Consistent with the *habitual* approaches to rejuvenation that many resilient people appear to have adopted is research done on the benefits of exercise by Daniel Landers of Arizona State University.[11] He found, among other things, that in order to reduce anxiety and depression, *regular* exercise (several weeks' worth) was more effectual than *isolated* physical activities. This jibes with my observation that many resilient people *integrate* their recharging behaviors, whatever they are, into their daily or weekly *routines*. Once we make the activities routine, they then bear *ongoing* and compounded fruits.

So how exactly does regular exercise achieve its well-publicized results? Though the science gets complicated (and is a bit above my pay grade), basically physical activity can boost energy by delivering oxygen and nutrients to your blood and brain, which in turn increases the overall efficiency of your cardiovascular system. As for mood relatively strenuous exercise facilitates the release of endorphins from the pituitary gland, thus encouraging positive emotional responses. This process is similar to the sunlight dynamic discussed earlier, and like sunlight, may have a basis in our evolution. Essentially, we receive positive reinforcement for our physicality in part because that activity was necessary to help us avoid becoming bipedal snacks out on the African savanna.

Perhaps the greatest testament to the value of exercise for those with lots on their plates is the fact that the last few residents of the White House each had their own regular exercise routines and preferences: the first Bush played tennis, Clinton jogged regularly (sometimes straight into McDonalds, but still), the second Bush liked to mountain bike, and the Obama's are celebrated for the time they spend in the gym (Barak Obama famously showed up to work out at seven o'clock the morning *after* he was elected leader of the free world the first time!). Even John F. Kennedy became an avid exerciser and was reportedly in the best shape of his life just prior to his untimely death.

Yoga

This ancient Indian form of spiritual/physical practice has increased significantly in popularity over the last few decades. Most forms involve physical stretching and poses, as well as concentrated breathing, mantras, and meditation. The term *yoga* comes from the Sanskrit word referring to "connection" and" joining." This sense of connection to the world's energy and our highest selves is a major goal of this practice and highly reflective of the rejuvenation phenomena we've been discussing. Other goals of yoga include cleansing of the spirit, raising consciousness, and increasing mindfulness and self-awareness.

An invaluable element of yoga, which is particularly relevant to our thinking on resilience, is its de-emphasis of the ego. Unlike most of our daily activities, yoga has as one of its primary goals the "loss of the self." Consequently, narcissism and ego are among its enemies. But even within the granola and Birkenstock world of yoga, competition, vanity, and ego cannot be fully eradicated. As yoga becomes more mainstream and finds its way into virtually every neighborhood gym, this anti-ego oasis may be in jeopardy.

In a *New York Times* op-ed piece,[12] the dean of the Graduate School of Holistic Studies at John F. Kennedy University in California, David Surrenda wrote, "many gyms that offer yoga emphasize the physical exercise without teaching the essential self-awareness that differentiates yoga from any exercise. The *narcissism*, which is not uncommon in many sports, is the result of an emphasis on exercise that misinterprets what the real intention of yoga practice is. Yes, one can increase muscle mass and decrease waist size, but that's not the real goal. Much of the yoga practiced today has actually become the antithesis of yoga as it is meant to be."

This de-emphasis of the self and subjugation of the ego are key reasons why and how yoga can be such an effective form of relaxation and regeneration, especially for those focused on resilience. Ultimately, like many of the activities we have covered, it provides an invaluable, if temporary, vacation from ourselves and more importantly our seemingly relentless stream of anxiety-inducing thoughts.

So, does yoga work? Well, it is difficult and perhaps arrogant to argue with literally thousands of years of anecdotal success. I would think that anything that has endured that long must have value, if for no other reason than it wouldn't have survived if not. Additionally, I'd figure that over the millennia any flaws would have been weeded out along the way as a result of its evolution. But, this would not be the first time I risked being called arrogant, so let's take a brief look at the research on yoga's efficacy.

A study sponsored by the American Council on Exercise,[13] and led by Dawn Boehde PhD and John Porcari, PhD, focused on the physical benefits of yoga and found that for the women in their study (average age thirty-three), yoga correlated with significant increases in balance, endurance, muscularity, and flexibility. This and other studies appear to support the anecdotal and historical claims for yoga related to physical fitness.

But what about our focus on stress reduction and improved mental outlook? Though it is difficult to operationalize and quantify these concepts, there does appear to be evidence, however, it is less robust than that for the physical benefits.

A 2010 study published in the *Journal of Biobehavioral Medicine*[14] and conducted by Ohio State University researchers found that yoga practice had not only appeared to decrease the amount of specific proteins linked to stress and aging (average age of participants was forty-one), but also that regular practitioners actually responded less severely to outside stressors than nonpractitioners. In other words it appeared that their practice helped make them more *physiologically resistant* to stress. This gets at the very essence of what it means to live resilience; doing things regularly that both increase one's stress resistance quotient and cultivating the skills necessary to respond if and when the stressors do break through.

Intimate and Honest Conversation

For many people the cathartic nature of intimate and honest conversation appears to meet their needs for physiological and emotional rejuvenation. Contrary to popular belief, a formal therapeutic context (i.e., therapist and patient) does not have to be present in order for there to be significant therapeutic benefit. Think about it, people have been sharing intimate truths with others and reaping the benefits long before Sigmund Freud and his introduction of psychoanalysis in the mid to late 1800s. And many believe that the first real psychologists were ancient Greek philosophers such as Plato and Aristotle. Whether it was to a clergyman, a sibling, a close friend, or a spouse, throughout history people have actively unburdened themselves, having loads lifted and spirits cleansed in the process.

The word catharsis comes from the Greek word *K'atharsis*, which refers to "a cleansing." This idea of cleansing the mind, thus refreshing the individual, captures the mechanism of how and why intimate and sincere conversations can have such profound and healthful effects. (In fact, if you are a practicing Catholic, vis-à-vis the Sacrament of Penance and confession, it could be the difference between spending eternity in heaven or hell.)

The idea of having someone to share with on a regular basis closely mirrors another element of resilience woven into so much of what we've discussed thus far, namely the need for assistance and support from others.

Going beyond resilience, having close relationships, and socializing with others have been identified as key correlates to living longer and more rewarding lives. Again, we can go back to evolution. The desire to socialize and cooperate with others is built into our DNA via natural selection. Interacting with others stimulates us at a genetic level and correspondingly is reinforced by positive emotions.

So what makes for good talking and listening, as well as talkers and listeners? Researchers from Southeast Missouri State University had ten expert counselors rank twenty-two personality characteristics as to their value for counselors[15]; among the most important were *empathy, acceptance,* and *warmth.* Closely related to these is what I have found to be the most important ingredient for promotion of resilience through interpersonal catharsis and regeneration: *absolute candidness.*

Like most precious things, honest and heartfelt interpersonal communication really is quite rare. If you think about your average day or week, how much of the time are you truly sharing your *honest* feelings, thoughts, and emotions? If you're like most people, it's probably a very small percentage. If we're lucky we have a close friend, spouse, partner or family member with whom we can really talk a few times a week. But most of the time, we keep the deeply personal, private (and ultimately most meaningful) stuff to ourselves. Usually this is because of feelings of vulnerability and/or fear of embarrassment. And this is a shame because often it's that stuff we're so afraid to express that we'd get the most out of sharing.

Far from sharing intimate truths, we are not only usually sharing lies (or at least lies of omission) in our conversations, but both sides usually know they are lies, and what's more, prefer it that way! If people went around actually telling the truth all the time it would make for many an uncomfortable moment.

Imagine you're at work tomorrow morning and your coworker Frank saunters in. You lift your head from your computer screen just slightly and mutter a perfunctory, "Hey, how ya doing?" To which Frank responds with an exasperated sigh and then, "Actually, I feel like crap. I suspect my wife is sleeping with the pool boy, I've been depressed for over six months now, which is about as long as I've been constipated, and what else…oh yeah, this morning my daughter told me she hates my guts and wishes that the pool boy was her dad instead of me." Most of us would cringe with embarrassment, or pretend not to hear him, or both. It is so rare that we simply do not expect openness and honesty in our daily lives, so when people are frank (pun intended) and sincere, it is often unsettling. Normally, if we disclose at all, we save it for the few people (again, if we're lucky) with whom we share closeness, intimacy, and rapport.

Lies and partial truths are such a part of our modern society that from a sociological perspective, a world without them would be scarcely recognizable. The 2009 film *The Invention of Lying* takes a comical look at just such a place. For whatever reason, the inhabitants of this land (except for the protagonist eventually) simply *cannot* lie. This leads to lots of hurt feelings, a lack of euphemisms, and some refreshing honesty. In this world, a retirement home is called "A Sad Place Where Homeless Old People Come to Die," and a Pepsi ad reads "For when they don't have Coke." This clever film highlights that fact that our society is awash in the apocryphal, the insincere, and the superficial. This is why deep authenticity, especially between people, is so rare and like most rare things, potentially valuable.

The need and value of honest intimacy is captured well by psychiatrist Lynn Ponton in her essay *Characteristics of Effective Counseling.*[16] She writes, "It's important that you and your counselor establish a good relationship that allows you to be completely honest about your thoughts and feelings. Often this requires an elusive "chemistry" between both of you in which you feel comfortable with your counselor's personality, approach, and style. If after the first few sessions you don't feel this chemistry, look for another counselor with whom you feel more comfortable."

The fact that the chemistry Ponton writes about is indeed "elusive" is precisely why so many people do not rely on professionals, but rather on friends and family (who are also cheaper come to think of it). Often these relationships have evolved over time and survive *precisely because* they have organically achieved high levels of the honesty and chemistry Ponton values.

Intimacy and honesty are two sides of the same coin, and it would be difficult to have one without the other. We have talked about the potential value of twelve-step programs such as Alcoholics Anonymous (AA) and Narcotics Anonymous (NA) which have survived for almost eighty years now based on the simple premise that people with grave and seemingly relentless addictions could heal by sharing their truths in safe and supportive communities.

An Australian study published in the *Journal of Epidemiol Community Health*[17] chronicled a ten-year longitudinal study which followed 1,477 people aged seventy and over and found that those with larger social networks (i.e., more friends) lived significantly longer. In this case at least, it appears that friends can actually prolong life.

Supporting the undervalued nature of friendship in our society, University of North Carolina sociologist Rebecca Adams believes that "In general, the role of friendship in our lives isn't terribly well appreciated...There is just scads of stuff on families and marriage but very little on friendship. It baffles me. Friendship has a bigger impact on our psychological well-being than family relationships."[18] Wow! Adams's final statement is a bold one that I am not sure I completely agree with, but whether or not it is more or less impactful than family, any way you slice it, friendship is still a big deal.

More closely related to how friendship can relate to resilience, particularly in how it can actually increase that all important attribute self-efficacy, is a fascinating study done by University of Virginia researchers.[19] This study found that not only does friendship empower, but it can actually *increase our perceptions of what we think we can accomplish.* Researchers brought students to the base of a steep hill and had them put on weighted backpacks. Some of the students stood next to their friends and others were alone. Those who were standing next to friends reported lower steepness estimates, while those who were alone estimated higher steepness. In other words *simply being with a friend* may increase ambition and confidence by making a challenge *appear* more doable. These researchers also found correlations between the degree of closeness of friendships and the perceived ease of the task. One of the study's authors, Dennis R. Preofitt, said, "What we are finding is that things that we have always thought of as having metaphorical value, like friendship, actually affect our physiology. Social support changes how we perceive the world and how our bodies work."

The bottom line is that we *need* others with whom we can share and on whom we can count. Whether these individuals are counselors, spouses, family members, or simply BFFs, for many they serve as invaluable resources for deep sharing, regeneration, and support.

Additional Examples of Charging Stations

The examples discussed heretofore are some of the more popular regenerative activities/resources that resilient people count on to stay sharp and replenish their energy levels so they can better manage the stressors in their lives. These restorative activities are consistent sources of strength and elasticity for our metaphorical rubber bands. Through them we increase our competence and capacity to engage in the three steps of the resilience formula.

Other examples of charging stations used to a lesser extent by people I have known or researched include the following:

- Frequent vacationing
- Relating to pets
- Practicing martial arts/tai chi
- Creating art

- Watching movies
- Collecting stamps
- Gardening
- Playing musical instruments
- Fishing/Hunting
- Sunbathing
- Motorcycle riding
- Attending support groups
- Playing videogames
- Visiting museums
- Getting massages
- Volunteer work

If you can already identify an activity or routine you practice that provides you with a spiritual and/or physical boost on a regular basis, my advice would be to not only continue with it, but consciously value what it is doing for you and how. And, if you deem it possible and potentially beneficial, increase the frequency with which you engage in this activity.

As you assess its value, think strategically about ways to maximize its efficacy. Perhaps there are certain types of stressors to which it responds more effectively than others, or there are times of the day or week that it appears to produce more positive results. The more intelligently you utilize your regeneration system, the better it will prepare you for your traumas, be they present already or lying in wait.

Making it Work for You

If you cannot identify something (or someone) you already have in your life that meets these rejuvenation criteria (or simply want to add more), then you may have to develop it yourself. You can start by reviewing the list of activities discussed above and asking yourself if any of them seem like ones you'd like to cultivate for yourself. If so you can use trial and error until one clicks.

If none of them jump out at you, don't get discouraged. Like meeting the right potential life partner, securing a meaningful career, or finding just the right shoes for that red dress, this is about the right match.

In order to spark some ideas, it may help to ponder the following questions with as much honesty and candor as possible:

- When, specifically, during my average week (or month) do I feel most whole and complete?
- At what point in my average week (or month) do I feel most energized and empowered?
- Is there any point in my average week (or month) when I feel a sense of *flow*, when time seems to lose its meaning and I am fully engaged in the moment?
- When in my average week (or month) am I most open and honest?
- Are there any activities or interests I enjoyed as a child that I might want to pick up again?
- If I had a week off, with no pressing responsibilities or deadlines, how would I spend that time?
- Are there any activities, hobbies, skills or pastimes that I have been wanting to learn more about but haven't?

In thinking about your responses, do you notice any themes or patterns? Are there types of activities, or places, or people that seem to keep rising to the surface? If so, use these recurring ideas to target some options.

As mentioned above, trial and error may be the way to go here. The well-known personal development guru Steve Pavlina promotes a "30-Day Trial" approach for testing and adopting new habits.[20] He commits wholeheartedly to a new habit or activity for thirty days, no matter how difficult or unrewarding it may seem initially. Once the thirty days have passed, he thoroughly and objectively evaluates the benefits (if any) and then decides if he will continue. According to Pavlina a valuable advantage of this approach is that it dodges any fear of commitment we may have. To say I will do X *forever* can be quite daunting (depending what X is I guess, if X = breathing, it may not be too difficult...but I digress), we may be defeated before we even begin. But to say I will do X for only a month provides a much needed escape hatch if things begin to go south.

Pavlina practices what he preaches and reports some intriguing results using the thirty-day trials for activities such as exercising daily, giving up television, and waking up at five in the morning. After trying vegetarianism for thirty days, he was so excited about the results that he then became a vegan. So commit fully to the one or more of the regenerative activities that appeal to you and monitor the results closely.

Characteristics of Quality Regenerative Activities

If you are still having difficulty *identifying* healthful regenerative activities though, it may be helpful to review some characteristics of quality ones.

- *Noncompetitive:* Remember, activities that stimulate the ego are usually not regenerative or peaceful. Competition by definition pits us against one another and creates a desire to "win." Consequently, if and when we "lose" (whatever losing is for us), we will simply become more anxious and disgruntled. Remember, for most of us, our egos are in play virtually all of our waking hours. Consequently, engaging in activities that help distance ourselves from them can be highly beneficial. However, if you are an excellent loser (in other words losing is no big deal to you) a competitive activity may be just fine.

- *Schedulable/Practical:* The reason many of the questions I asked you to ponder above had "in your average week (or month)" in them is because, if possible, I wanted you to identify activities that were *already* part of your life. These are more likely to fit within your schedule and lifestyle, and thus are more practical. For example, maybe you love skiing, but if you live in Arizona, you may not be able to schedule it into your routine. Remember, the more practical something is, the more likely it is that you will repeatedly do it.

- *Sociable/Solitary:* I know this one sounds like a cop out (Should it be sociable or solitary? Make up your mind!), but I think it depends. Conventional wisdom is that if you are an introvert (i.e., you get energized by being alone), then you should do solitary acts; and vice versa if you are an extravert. However, you may also want to think about how social you are in your daily life. If you have a job or lifestyle where you are constantly talking to others and surrounded by people (e.g., receptionist, police officer, nurse, therapist, etc.), then you may benefit from doing more solitary activities, because that would be more of a mental vacation for you. However, if you spend lots of quiet time alone (e.g., writer/ researcher, artist, accountant, computer programmer, etc.) then an activity with more social contact may be just what the doctor ordered. The bottom line is that you want to think about activities that would help promote *balance* in your life.

- *Authentic:* Here I will *not* be on the fence. In fact there really is no "fence" to speak of— just a wide open field. Your regenerative activity *must* provide you with time to be your bona fide you. Not only should you feel validated but also connected to a deeper part of yourself and the world. The fostering of this sense of authenticity is the one characteristic that, in one way or another, was shared by all of the regenerative activities discussed previously. For some reason, exploring and connecting with our essential natures not just feels good but nurtures something precious within us.

- *Fun:* Do not underestimate the value of enjoyment. Aside from the obvious fun of having fun, the more we enjoy an activity the more likely it is that we will continue to do it.

It should be noted that many people do not rely on one major regenerative activity, but rather take more of a smorgasbord (try spelling that without Google!) approach to meeting the objective.

By consistent recharging, we can increase the likelihood that we can handle the crisis rather than it handling us.

CHAPTER 6:
ROGER, LUZ, AND YOU WORK THE FORMULA

For years I've been convinced that someone, or something, had been stealing and hiding one sock from every pair I purchased. What this thing's motive or rationale was, I have no idea. But no matter what I did, once those socks went into the laundry, only one from each pair would emerge. It was like they went into the woods for a duel, boldly declaring "Sir, only one of us shall return!" It was insane. Fed up one day, I bought ten pairs of the same exact socks—black with gold colored toes. This worked for a while, but after a few weeks, I could not find *any* matching pairs. All I could conclude was that the sock monsters had a personal vendetta against me.

Then one night I was watching some standup comedian, and he was joking about the *same exact thing*. So it wasn't just me! Apparently sock monsters were targeting others as well. Though I still had trouble finding matching socks, the realization did come as somewhat of a relief. Something I thought was so specific to me was actually somewhat universal.

And, I realized, it went beyond socks. I'm not the only one who screams and curses like a madman at customer service recordings. I'm not the only one who thinks the long list of side effects at the end of prescription drug commercials is absurd. I'm not the only one whose wife makes him complete chores before he can watch the big game (Am I?). I'm not the only one who can't tell the difference between the Kardashian sisters. And I'm not the only one who hates having the sheets tucked in tight at a hotel. These are all experiences/thoughts that I believed to be unique to me, but which, apparently, are shared with many of my fellow human beings.

It's a strange paradox; as individuals we are exceedingly unique, yet astonishingly similar. Stand-up comedians like Jerry Seinfeld and Chris Rock make entire careers by pointing out things we thought only we experienced but are actually quite universal.

So what does this have to do with resilience? It is a reminder that while we are all individuals and caught up in the minutia and drama of the particulars of our daily lives, simultaneously we share *so* much, often more than I think we realize. Consequently, taking a closer look at the specifics of how other individuals have managed to live resilience can not only inspire us but help us see the potential resilience in ourselves.

As testament to the preeminence of context and the real world, what follows are relatively detailed stories of individuals utilizing the tenants of the resilience formula in the process of practicing their own versions of resilience. It is hoped that by seeing the resilience formula in action, you will gain a greater understanding of its potential practical value for you.

Roger Works It

It was the stench he remembers most: body odor, sweat, slightly sour milk, and fear, lots of fear. It all combined to create an odor unlike anything he'd experienced before. Perhaps it was because he had been trapped, literally, with those smells, powerless to do anything about them, that they'd remained in his olfactory system even months after he was released.

It all felt like an ornate lie or an alternative universe or it had all happened to someone else. Just thinking the words seemed like the start of some sort of fiction: "I was in jail." *What the hell happened?* Roger thought.

This was not supposed to happen to people like me—educated people with jobs and mortgages! But happen it did.

Roger had been, by almost any account, a successful man. And not only did he know it, unlike many others he didn't take it for granted. He had been a well-respected school psychologist in an urban middle school—extremely well liked by the students and admired by the staff and administration alike. He had a reputation for being highly effective with the kids, not only helping them understand and address their issues but connecting them with appropriate school and community resources as well. Parents of the students loved him; before every winter break he'd be showered with homemade baked goods and five dollar gift cards to Dunkin Donuts in appreciation of his good works.

Roger married a lovely and compassionate woman, Linda, he had met in grad school a decade earlier, and they had a six-year-old daughter they named Lucy after his deceased mother. Combining his salary with what Linda made as a social worker, the two were able to afford a small but comfortable home in a safe, somewhat prosperous, middle-class suburban neighborhood. They even had the white picket fence they'd both always wanted. Life was as close to perfect as the real world could get until a relatively minor car accident changed everything.

Driving home from work on a snowy night in late December— brownies, cupcakes and gift cards in tow—Roger lost control of his SUV and careened into the highway divider. Airbags did deploy, but his knee slammed into the bottom portion of the dashboard, causing a fracture to the kneecap.

The sharp and chronic pain was almost unbearable, thus while in the hospital he had been given copious amounts of prescription pain killers. Six months later he found himself continuing to take them even though most of the physical pain had subsided. "I don't really *need* to take them," he told himself, "but my knee does still hurt a bit."

When Linda would inquire if he was still taking the pills, Roger, afraid she'd lose respect for him or think he had a problem, would say no. Before he knew it, he found himself stashing bottles of pills in furtive but accessible locations—under the seat of his car, in his locked desk drawer at work, and in the aspirin bottle in the pocket of his winter parka hanging in the closet.

As weeks and months passed, the idea of getting through the day without his pills became more and more daunting. Regardless, he remained convinced he could stop if he *really* wanted to, and he would when the time was right, "probably next week or month sometime."

Eventually, his doctor, realizing there might be a problem, stopped writing him prescriptions. "Just stick to Advil," he'd said. With this Roger found himself going to other doctors, exaggerating the pain in his knee and seeking more prescriptions. Many would see through the facade, but enough wouldn't, and he was able to keep the pills coming in.

Meanwhile, both his work and marriage began to suffer. First gradually, almost imperceptibly, then in more and more overt ways. At work he found it difficult to pay attention to the students' issues; his mind continuously drifted to how and where he could get more pills. And on days when he only had a few remaining, he'd become irritable and lose patience with his students and their seemingly "endless grumblings."

The impatience and irritability followed him home. He snapped at his daughter if she didn't eat all her vegetables or left the orange juice out. So caught up in his scheming to get more pills, he showed less and less interest in Linda and what was going on in her life.

Linda would ask what was wrong, and he'd reply, "Nothing, I'm just tired." However, being a trained therapist herself, she sensed something more going on. But when she pressed him, he'd snap at her and accuse her of making things up and "nagging him incessantly." For the first time since they'd met she began seriously contemplating a future apart from him.

One night she noticed him slurring his words during dinner and then falling asleep right at the dining room table. The next morning she confronted him: "Roger, you *need* to tell me what the hell is going on. Are you taking something?" Not only did Roger deny he was taking anything or that anything was wrong, he reprimanded her for even asking.

Still not convinced she gave it one more try: "Roger, I love you and want to make this work. I can see you're not yourself. You *need* to tell me what's going on, or I don't know if I can keep this going." Roger responded with words he'd end up regretting more than almost anything else, "Linda, I swear on Lucy's life there is *nothing* going on. I've just been working too hard. I'm tired, that's all, I swear."

Roger began calling in sick to work more and more frequently. Despite long lists of students craving his guidance and waiting to see him, Roger spent his sick days making appointments at medical offices and clinics as far as one hundred miles away and seeing as many doctors as possible. Eventually, he ran out of doctors who would even take his calls, let alone write him a script.

Roger was at a loss. He couldn't imagine facing the day sober but was quickly running out of options. He then made one of those critical and fateful decisions that dramatically alter the trajectory of a person's life.

On one of his countless "sick days," he drove into the city where he worked and made his way into a housing project where many of his students lived. He began asking around—if anyone was selling pills. The obvious risk of being seen by someone who knew him was nowhere near as significant to Roger as his increasingly sole motivation—getting more pills.

Roger continued soliciting the people hanging out in front of the apartment buildings and corner stores, asking if they were "holding." After four or five incredulous looks, he finally found someone who responded positively. At first the dealer asked if he was the police, and after several protestations finally said, "Wait here. I'll be right back."

Roger waited anxiously, hoping he was not going to get ripped off. Not so much out of fear of losing his money but because he would then have to find another dealer. A few minutes later, the guy came back with a paper bag and asked for "fifty." Uncertain what was in the bag, but too eager to question, he gave the dealer two twenties and a ten. The dealer palmed the money and walked briskly away.

Roger too hurried off, and after taking several quick steps, opened the bag. *Yes!* he thought, seeing the bag was filled with pills, *My worries are over, at least for a little while.* But at that exact moment, a loud voice drowned out his thoughts, not yelling, but extraordinarily forceful and commanding: "Police! Don't fucking move!"

What happened next was more a bad dream than anything resembling reality…Handcuffs, reading of rights, head pushed down upon entering the backseat of a police cruiser…It did not compute. It was like watching a movie but being in it at the same time.

There was more of the bad dream: police station, fingerprints, booking, and then perhaps the worst part of all…the phone call.

Roger had no lawyer, never really needed one. He thought of who to call, and though it would be the most difficult call of his life, he knew it had to be Linda.

She reacted slowly, as if not comprehending his words, but once her disbelief and anger dissipated, she finally agreed to secure a lawyer.

Roger spent a sleepless night in jail with barely enough room to sit, let alone recline onto his back. After seeing the judge, he was released the next day on bail brought by Linda and an attorney she found in the yellow pages.

In the weeks and months that followed, his arrest was written up in the local newspaper, he was fired from his job, and he separated from his wife. The man who had had everything, and knew it, had lost it all, and knew that too.

In exchange for a guilty plea and an agreement to enter a drug rehabilitation program, the charges for the first-time offender were reduced from purchasing narcotics to simple possession. He was to go directly to the rehabilitation center where he was to successfully complete a ninety-day program. Additionally, he would need a positive report from the center's staff, demonstrating that he was drug free and as fully "recovered" as one could be.

Upon entering the rehab center, further surrealism—bags checked for contraband, cell phone confiscated, strip-searched, anal cavity searched… utter humiliation. He was treated like a *real* addict and criminal, not a victim of circumstances, which was what he really was.

Detox was followed by buprenorphine and other medications to mitigate withdrawal, which would then be followed by intensive behavioral therapy, both group and individual.

For the first three weeks, Roger *said* all the right things but didn't believe much of what was so effortlessly spewing forth. Being a psychologist himself, he not only felt superior to everyone there, but he knew what he was supposed to say and what he wasn't. His plan was to give them what they wanted and get the hell out of there.

While sitting in group and listening to the residents' stories, he couldn't shake the notion that the whole thing was a big misunderstanding, that he didn't really belong there, that he wasn't *really* an addict (*It was prescription pills for Christ's sake! Not cocaine or heroin!*) and definitely not a criminal.

At the beginning of each group session, he had to introduce himself with, "My name is Roger, and I'm an addict." But repeating it over and over again made it feel like no less of a lie.

A month into his stay, Roger was assigned a new counselor, Carl. Roger had seen him in the group sessions before but thought he was a former resident or an observer or security or something. The guy looked like no counselor he'd ever seen. He looked more like a Hell's Angel than anything else. First off, he was big, at least six feet four and wide all over. Not really fat, just thick everywhere, like a side of raw beef. And his cloths! He wore dark jeans, clunky black work boots, a long sleeve black shirt, and a brown vest of crackled leather. His face was all hair. He had a thick salt-and-pepper moustache that dropped down at the edges and connected to a shaggy beard that hung to the top of his barrel chest. His eyebrows were an unkempt mess of shag as well, but his head was completely bald, with strange knobs protruding here and there.

Initially, the new counselor was intimidating, but once the shock wore off, Roger was pretty confident he'd be able to schmooze him as well.

Carl began with, "Roger, I'm going to ask you a simple question. Why are you here?"

Roger responded with a well-rehearsed spiel: "My addiction is a disease, and my disease took over. I'm powerless over this disease, but if I continue to work the steps, I know I can make it. I need to surrender to my higher power."

Carl looked at him dubiously but didn't say anything. He then made a note on his pad and looked back at Roger. "Roger," he said, "I think you're full of shit."

Stunned and taken aback, Roger replied, "What are you talking about? You do know I'm a psychologist right? Did they tell you that?"

Carl just shook his head.

The two met every day for at least an hour, and each time Roger came up with a new shtick in attempts to appease the big guy and get him to lay off. But none of it worked. "You're still BS-ing me," is about all Carl would say.

Eventually, the residents were allowed to make a limited number of phone calls to the outside world, but each and every time Roger called Linda, he would get voicemail. And while he'd left messages, he received none that she'd called back.

With the realization that he may have lost his family for good, Roger fell into an even deeper despondency. Losing his career, and the embarrassment—those things hurt, but they were not fatal blows. The notion that Linda and Lucy were moving on without him, that was too much to take.

The sessions with Carl remained prolonged periods of mostly silence. Roger had run out of gambits and was losing faith in his ability to convince Carl that he really didn't belong here, that all he needed was a positive report and he'd then get on with his life.

"I'm not going to *make* you talk," Carl would say. So they'd sit in silence, listening to the large clock tick softly.

At the end of the fifth week, as the two remained locked in their daily staring contest, Carl finally broke in, "Roger, do you think you're better than the people here?"

Roger was about to say, "No, of course not. I'm not *better* than anyone." But he stopped himself. He thought about Linda and Lucy moving away—Linda remarrying, Lucy calling someone else, "Dad." He felt a curious pressure build up behind his eyes, one he hadn't felt in what seemed like forever. Try as he did to suck them back in, it was no use; and once the tears began, he couldn't stop them. Roger closed his eyes, leaned over, and cradled his face in his hands.

He wept and wept, then wept some more. He was too ashamed to lift his head. He feared the look that would be on Carl's face—a look of self-satisfaction, of smugness—a look that said, *I finally got you, you arrogant little snob. Still think you're better than us?*

But when he finally craned his neck and peered through saline-soaked fingers, what he saw was the most compassionate and empathetic face he could have imagined. Carl was offering him a tissue with one hand and reaching out to pat him on the shoulder with the other. "It's OK, man. Just let it out. It's OK, man, it really is," is all he kept saying.

Silence ceased being an issue. Roger and Carl talked and talked, often going beyond the allotted time. And though he still fought it at times, Roger came to some pretty sobering conclusions: his being here was not a mistake or a bad dream. Not a clerical error, not an overreaction by the justice system, and not a perfect storm of unfortunate events. Tough as it was, he had to admit he was there because of him in general, and his arrogance and ego in particular. He thought he was immune to the trials and tribulations faced by others, and that falling prey to drugs and addictive behavior was something that happened to those less evolved "masses." He thought he could handle things on his own, doing it his way—that the laws of nature and society somehow didn't really apply to him, essentially, that he was *above it all*... How wrong he was. "Look around," Carl would say. "This is no mistake, and it's definitely not a fucking dream."

Like his confidence and faith, Roger's willingness to admit culpability would come and go. At times he was able to see himself, his actions, and their consequences as valid and logical outcomes of one another, but often he would fall back into the comfortable position of "I don't really belong here. If anything, I should be *doing* the counseling, not getting it... This is a waste of time."

As Carl insisted, Roger shared virtually all of his thoughts, even the unflattering ones. And to his credit, Carl did not reprimand, chastise, or lecture. As long as he sensed Roger being honest, he'd usually respond with, "It's OK, man. It really is."

At Carl's suggestion Roger began keeping a journal. "You're a very cognitive person," he had told Roger. "And while lots of times that's a good thing, when it comes to recovery, thinking can sometimes get you in trouble. It has the potential of making that which is straightforward and simple muddled and complex. So write down everything in your journal— that can be your intellectual outlet. Get all that stuff down there, so when you're not writing, you can be present and open." So write Roger did, and within a week he needed another notebook.

Roger began feeling a degree of levity and optimism about life he had not felt since before the accident. And with that levity came the return of a level of physical energy he had not remembered having since he was in college. The rehab center had an old but reasonably well-stocked gym, and Roger began hitting it six days a week. Free weights, treadmill, elliptical machine, Nautilus, he did it all. At first it was as a release for his newfound energy, but strangely, as he continued he found it was both a release *and* generator of energy. Though far from the purpose of his stay, Roger ended up losing ten pounds and building a decent amount of physical stamina and new muscle.

When Roger began mentoring many of the new residents, both he and Carl knew that something fundamental had shifted in Roger's outlook. He'd provide the newbies with practical information, *stay away from so and so, Tuesday is chili dog night in the cafeteria, don't be late for group meetings*, etc., as well as emotional guidance and support in the form of timeworn but useful counsel: *Keep working the program. It works if you work it. Once you admit you are powerless, healing can begin. One day at a time. Surrender.*

At their last session, Roger and Carl once again talked of the future, and despite the plans they'd cultivated, Roger's enthusiasm and faith again began to wane. He knew he would get a glowing report and that he'd be "free." But free for what? "The thing is," began Roger, "I've lost everything. I'm such a royal screw-up! Getting my family back is the priority, and who knows how that'll go. But that's not it. I mean, I now have a freakin' *criminal* record *and* have been through drug rehab. I *know* people look down at those things because I did myself. I mean, let's be real—I won't be able to get a good job. I'm sure my previous colleagues will write me off, forget about any references from them. I'm not even exactly sure where I'll even be *living* long-term. My brother said I can stay on his couch for a while, but after that I'll be freakin' homeless!" And on and on went Roger.

When Roger's rant finally came to an apparent end, Carl said, "Are you done, or is there more?" Roger said nothing. "The fact is," Carl continued, "all of those crappy possibilities you've just spewed are only that, *possibilities*. You have no idea what will happen when you leave here, but consistent with your tendency toward arrogance, you're certain that you do. You want my advice? Slow down and look at the facts, but only the facts: like literally millions of Americans, you suffer from an addiction, and as part of that addiction you broke a law—a law that many believe should not even be, but a law nonetheless—and were arrested. You are now in the process of taking responsibility for that addiction and your actions, which is why you are here. That's it, no more and no less. Anything else this might "mean" is up to you. So slow down with all of this the sky is falling shit. *You're an accomplished man. That doesn't disappear just because you took a left turn when you should have gone right. . .Figure out what's really important to you, and go get it!*"

A week later Roger found himself unable to sleep and sitting at his brother's kitchen table at two in the morning. Earlier that day he'd finally spoken to Linda. She did say that he *said* all the right things, but she also knew how good he was at *saying* them. She spoke of broken trust and anger and resentment, and despite Roger's hopes, she concluded that she was "not even close to ready" to taking him back. However, she did agree to having him come over on Saturday to see Lucy. And that was something at least.

In thinking it through, he realized that his inability to sleep was due as much to excitement as anything else. Yes, he was disappointed that she did not want him back, but she *had* said, "not even close," which meant that there was still hope—there was indeed *possibility*. If not she would have used more definitive words like "never," "absolutely not," and, one of her favorites, "no way on hell."

Figure out what's really important to you, and go get it. With Carl's words still ringing in his head, Roger began writing in his journal. What was important to him was easy: first was his family and next his reputation, but *how* to go about getting them was much more difficult.

Roger came to two major conclusions. The first brought hope and the second dread. First, he realized getting what he wanted most would require getting what he wanted second most. If he could prove himself worthy of being a changed man (i.e., get his reputation back), then it was likely Linda would at least give him a shot at getting back into her and Lucy's lives on a more permanent basis. But second, he realized this would take a long time and require something he often struggled with, patience.

Like most American men, Roger viewed himself as a man of action, a *speak first ask questions later* type of guy. He liked to diagnosis a problem, fix it, and move on. And while he was able to tell his clients/students, when he had them, that real, lasting change was gradual and took time, the reality was that he struggled with that himself. But there was no way around it, no short cut here. Winning back the respect and trust of his wife and professional colleagues would be a painstakingly slow and deliberate process. But again he heard Carl's words, "You're an accomplished man. That doesn't disappear because you took a left turn when you should have gone right."

The next day, after his morning exercise routine, he settled into a coffee shop booth and refined his daily, weekly, and monthly "To Do" lists. Many of the first items involved reaching out to people. Phone this person to apologize and explain and that one to inquire about work opportunities, etc. Professionally speaking he had to make certain that people knew he still had a license and that his difficulties, the legal ones at least, were essentially over.

Adding to the challenge was that he was still technically an addict. He reminded himself of what he'd heard over and over. Once an addict always an addict, weather recovering, active user, or somewhere in flux. And while he didn't have a strong desire to use again, he learned from the countless relapsers at rehab that one had to remain hypervigilant, that our addictions are always lurking, waiting for an opportunity to pounce. The to-do list here was pretty short, and had been prescribed by Carl and the folks at the rehab center: (a) don't pick up, (b) ninety NA meetings in ninety days, and (c) get a sponsor. It was a short list but an absolute prerequisite to meeting his larger objectives.

His to-do lists turned into daily routines, with most of his time parceled between working out, NA meetings, and professional networking.

Initially much of his enthusiasm was consumed by unexpected setbacks. Several people would not take his calls, and those who did *said* the right things but never got back to him with promised leads and feedback. Apparently word of his troubles had spread through the local mental health community like wild fire. *Stay away from Roger—would you want a drug addict who had been in prison in your school?* Ironically, even those who were supposed to understand and empathize with addicts and who purportedly bought into the notion that people *could* change and overcome their pasts did not give him the benefit of the doubt.

Roger's mood was buoyed however by getting to spend an entire half of a Saturday with Linda and Lucy. The three ate together, read storybooks, and went out for ice cream. Lucy seemed to treat him as if he hadn't been gone at all (she was basically told the truth—*Daddy was sick and had to go to a hospital to get better*), and Linda, on the outside at least, treated him reasonably well. While it broke his heart to have to leave their well-appointed and comfortable home for his brother's sparsely furnished apartment and lumpy couch, the mere *possibility* that he could get them back permanently motivated him to keep at it.

Financial stress was another layer of clouds looming. He had decent savings and an IRA he could tap into, but those were finite resources that could not be counted on long-term. For now the mortgage was getting paid each month, but without some extra income relatively soon, Linda would begin worrying about the house. And this was the *last* thing Roger wanted. The argument he was trustworthy which warranted his coming home would not be bolstered by a stack of unpaid bills. Even if it wasn't much, contributing something to the home should enhance his chances of returning.

With his career search sputtering for who knew how long, Roger needed *something*, even if it was only temporary. It had been years since he had worked in a field other than mental health, but he knew the bigger problem was going to be his ego. How could he go from a respected and esteemed adolescent psychologist to a minimum wage clock puncher? He thought again of Linda and Lucy and the home they'd built together, and with that he resolved to do whatever it took.

Upon returning to his favorite café with the classifieds and laptop in tow, he noticed an old fashioned *Help Wanted* sign perched on the windowsill. Three days later he began learning the ins and outs of brewing gourmet coffee.

So there Roger worked, five days a week, while continuing to put out feelers for counseling jobs. There was no luck yet with full-time positions, but he did land part-time work doing psychological- and learning-disability testing for a private consulting company. The two income sources produced enough money to keep Linda from worrying about the mortgage with enough left over to pay his brother a modest amount of rent.

One morning while working in the café, he noticed a friend from graduate school whom he hadn't seen in years seated at the counter. Not knowing what else to do, he hastily told his coworker he didn't feel well, grabbed his stomach, and quickly scampered to the bathroom.

As he hid in the bathroom like a child afraid of a ghost, he began thinking of Carl. He thought of what Carl would say if he saw him there, about the disappointment that would be written all over his face, about how Carl would think "this freaking guy has not learned a damn thing."

Guilt and shame fought, with guilt emerging the victor. Roger flushed the toilet as a means of keeping up the facade and marched out toward the counter to face the music. He then breathed a sigh of relief upon noticing the empty stool where his friend had been seated. He was relieved but also now certain of at least one thing—the next time he would not hide. *He was an accomplished man. That doesn't disappear because he took a left turn when he should have gone right.* Does it?

Roger soldiered on. He exercised early in the morning then worked at the cafe then went to NA meetings and did psychological testing most afternoons. During the NA meetings, he worked his way through the steps continuously and found them to be invaluable sources of soul- searching and self-realization. It was one of the few times in his day where he could really exhale and be himself, warts and all.

Along the way he picked up an NA sponsor, an older gentleman, Jack, who had been clean for twenty-three years. Jack was much more quiet and reserved than Carl, but the two, who it turned out were close friends themselves, shared a no-nonsense, brass-tacks approach to recovery that Roger seemed to respond to well.

Jack had only two requirements, but they were unconditional:

1. No using
2. Absolute honesty

Roger could live with that.

Meanwhile, Roger was impressing his supervisors at the psychological consulting company. Clients would provide glowing evaluations of his work, and potential clients began asking for him by name. After six weeks there, he had as much work as he could handle and combined with his work at the café was making almost as much as he had been making as a school psychologist, though without the health and retirement benefits. But far from satisfied, Roger continued sending out résumés and cover letters for open school psychologist positions and going for interviews on the rare occasions when they actually invited him to do so.

Initially, his determination to return to the counseling field was fueled by ego and the desire to reacquire the respect and admiration he felt he'd lost. And to an extent, that did remain a factor. But more and more he felt guilty about the students he'd let down from his previous job, and though he knew *that* particular bridge had been burnt to cinders, helping other students may, at least partially, assuage that guilt.

Six months after leaving rehab, Roger was in a pretty good place. His evolving to-do lists and journals now filled five notebooks, and Linda was impressed with the sincerity and consistency he'd demonstrated since his return. Their Saturday afternoon visits gradually evolved into overnight stays and then into entire weekends together. They even agreed on a trial period of his moving back in. Roger could not have been happier. Or so he thought.

Almost exactly a year after returning from rehab, he received two particularly noteworthy phone calls at almost exactly the same time. The first was from a principal and was a job offer to serve as school psychologist at a high school in a neighboring town. Apparently, Roger's supervisors at the consulting company could not have been more complimentary about him and had specifically pointed to his professionalism, character, and compassion as key attributes. Roger was thrilled about the job offer but was even more satisfied with once again hearing those words attached to his name.

As he was discussing the details of the position, Roger's iPhone blinked that he had another call. Normally he would have pressed "Ignore," but he recognized the number as coming from the rehab center where he'd spent three months, and curiosity got the better of him. He quickly asked the principal if he could call him right back and then clicked over.

It was Carl. After a few pleasantries and a quick game of catch up, he got down to why he'd called. Apparently he had been keeping tabs on Roger's progress, mostly through Jack, and was both pleased and impressed. Carl said, "Here's the thing Roger. We're opening another facility, an intensive outpatient program specifically for adolescent addicts, and the guy who was supposed to run it is moving to Florida...Anyway, we'd like to know if you're interested."

Roger didn't understand. "Interested in what?"

"In the position," said Carl. "You'd probably have to take some more classes and get your substance-abuse counselor certificate, but you could start on a provisional basis. I've told the higher -ups all about you and all you've done, and, yes, they'd like to meet you first, but those are basically formalities. They trust me, and I trust you...Let me know when you'd like to come in, and we can talk salary and details."

Luz Works It

While most girls her age were playing with Barbie dolls or pretending to be princesses, Luz was devouring the complete works of Jane Austen (according to Luz, the Harry Potter series was "inane and childish fluff"). While other girls had to be reminded to clean their rooms and do their homework, Luz kept a checklist next to her small desk so she'd never forget to do anything. And while most children dreaded getting a letter or phone call from school, Luz looked forward to the compliments and commendations they'd be sure to convey.

By the time she entered middle school, it was a statement of obvious fact that Luz was special. Although, or perhaps because, she grew up in a low-income neighborhood, she was tagged very early on as an academically gifted child—a child who, if she played her cards right and steered clear of the usual land mines littering her neighborhood, was certainly on her way up and perhaps more importantly, out. So many teachers, administrators, church officials, and family members pinned their hopes to her that they even held potluck fundraisers to cover any expenses not included in whatever college scholarships she'd be certain to be awarded. Luz was the "It girl." That person who gives everyone around her hope that there just might really be magic in the world.

Viewing Luz's giftedness as akin to winning the lottery, her mother, Rosemarie, closely orchestrated every aspect of Luz's life. Upon first realizing how exceptionally bright Luz was, Rosemarie saw it as her mission to *ensure* that, no matter what, she become successful. It was as much her dream as Luz's, perhaps even more so.

Rosemarie's vision of success could be defined as much by what it wasn't as what it was: *success* meant a college degree, not just a high school diploma; a career and not just a job; a house and not just an apartment; and a husband, not just being a single parent struggling alone. Like so many parents, she wanted for her daughter all that she never had.

Rosemarie's mission engendered an almost compulsive supervision of Luz's activities. Aside from Luz going to school and when Rosemarie had to work late at the supermarket, she rarely let Luz out of her sight. No playdates with friends, no afternoons hanging out at the park, no shopping downtown, and definitely no loitering in front of the bodega with those going-nowhere hoodlums—nothing. *Nothing* and nobody would stand in the way of Luz's making it.

Though she never told anyone, Rosemarie viewed Luz's virtually certain success as a ticket out for two. She had a vision of Luz as a professional woman, a lawyer perhaps, married with two children (one boy and one girl), living in a large center-hall colonial with a huge green lawn in the suburbs—a house so big that there'd be plenty of room for

Rosemarie, perhaps even a smaller house out back, next to a massive shade tree. Rosemarie could see the possibility. And with every passing year of Luz's achievement, that possibility became more and more real.

Rosemarie forced herself into just about every aspect of Luz's life. But as so often is the case, as Luz got older, resentment began to creep in. About the time she hit her midteens, Luz began challenging what she viewed as her mother's unreasonably dictatorial parenting style. In turn Rosemarie resented what she viewed as a lack of gratitude on Luz's part. And because they were both absolutely certain of being right, a constant tension began to characterize almost all of their interactions.

Unlike those of most parents like her, Rosemarie's unreasonably high standards were almost always met. Luz was one of those rare creatures destined for excellence because they are both naturally bright *and* work harder than most everyone else. Throughout three years in middle school, she earned nothing less than a ninety-nine on anything, and in high school she took virtually all honors courses and still graduated with a 4.0 GPA— of course she was her graduating class's valedictorian.

Increasing the salivation of college recruiters nationwide was that not only was she a brilliant minority female from a single-parent home who excelled academically, but she also flourished in the increasingly treasured realm of extracurriculars: student-counsel president—check; cocaptain of the softball team—check; cofounder and vice-president of the school's first environmental club—check. She was also an active peer mentor, charged with helping other students be successful.

In her role as student-counsel president and peer mentor, she was often asked to speak to younger female students, warning and advising them against just about everything: not only the dangers and consequences of unprotected sex, but drinking and drugs as well. When doing this she tried to come off as a "peer," as an equal, as one of them, but in a moment of honesty, she would have admitted to feeling apart from them, even a little better. When she'd see the inevitable two or three girls each year who'd waddle down the school's hallways with their protruding bellies, she couldn't help but stick her nose up the slightest bit. How could they be so stupid?

Luz could literally not wait to go away to college, taking summer and advanced-placement classes to graduate early. She knew she'd have options to stay close, but she was determined to get some distance between her and her overbearing mother. *What more did this woman want?* Luz thought. *How much more perfect can I be?*

Luz leveraged her obsessive perfection and manic work ethic and earned a virtual full-ride academic scholarship to a prestigious private university over two hundred miles away from her increasingly suffocating neighborhood and mother. And though her mother begged and pleaded with her to stay home and commute somewhere closer, Luz (convinced that was her mother's way of continuing her oppressive reign) refused.

Upon arriving at her dorm room for the first time, she remembers peering out the window at the finely manicured and stately grounds and thinking, *now* this *is where I belong.*

She had been warned that college classes would be much tougher (and they were) and that she would have to work even harder (and she did), but she still managed to excel. It seemed that her future was unfolding just as she (and her mother) had planned.

It was the first semester of her sophomore year, and midterms were just about over. Consequently, parties seemed to be popping up everywhere on campus. Luz had just finished taking her last exam, and for the first time in literally forever, she was unsure of how she did. Unaccustomed to this type of uncertainty, she felt the need to do something about it. So when her roommate Christy perfunctorily asked if Luz wanted to go to a fraternity party, she responded with an uncharacteristic, "Sure, why not."

During that evening Luz would do two things she'd never done before. And her life would change forever.

While at the party, Luz did the first thing she'd never done before: she got drunk. The most she ever drank prior to that night was a glass of wine and a few sips of beer—on that night she'd had six cups of punch spiked with grain alcohol. The drinks accomplished their goal of loosening her up, and she found herself speaking with a handsome exchange student from Costa Rica, named Alejandro, whom she'd never seen before.

The two talked about their hobbies and interests, and to Luz's surprise and delight, he was majoring in environmental science. To her further surprise, his English was excellent and the two talked and danced and then talked some more, and before she knew it, he was leading her by the hand toward a dark back room. It was there that Luz did the second thing she'd never done before: she had sex with someone she'd just met.

The next thing she remembered, it was quiet, the only sound was the pounding of her head. She was vomiting in a toilet and was still at the fraternity house. Dazed, disoriented, and suddenly alone, she'd managed to stumble her way out of the house and back to her dorm. She woke up in the lounge with several of her suitemates giggling at her uncharacteristically disheveled state. She then crawled into her room and bed and slept until it was dark.

Waking up again, this time with a massive and pounding headache, Luz was more ashamed and embarrassed than she'd thought possible. When people asked what had happened and where she'd been, she refused to answer. She spent the rest of that evening under her covers crying. When Christy repeatedly asked what was wrong, Luz would just cry some more and eek out a muffled "nothing."

After a week Luz began to feel like herself again. It was a crazy night, but it was over. And luckily and peculiarly for such a relatively small campus, she hadn't run into Alejandro. While she barely remembered his face, given the combination of alcohol and strobe lighting, she was still sure she'd recognize him.

As it turned out, she never did see him again and probably never would because as far as she could tell, he wasn't a student there. After some checking she found out there were no exchange students from Costa Rica, and a quick search of the university student database determined no current, or former for that matter, students named Alejandro.

At the time Luz was both angry and relieved. Angry that she'd been lied to and duped (*Sure* he was an environmental science major! No wonder his English was so good!) but relieved that she would not have to face him again. She felt as if she'd dodged a major bullet, and made a solemn oath to herself that she would never, ever, do anything like that again. And as the weeks passed, she'd all but forgotten about the silver-tongued bogus exchange student from Costa Rica. Unfortunately, however, Luz had not dodged the bullet. She was just unaware of being hit.

Luz was never late. Not for class, not for the shuttle bus that took her to class, not for doctor's appointments, not for church on the few occasions she would actually go—never. But something was definitely up. Normally she was clockwork, every twenty-eight days, but here it was almost five weeks, and no period.

Not in a million years would she have thought that she'd long for the cramps, bloating, headaches, and mood swings she'd dreaded every month. Yet there she was, literally praying they'd come already. She tried to convince herself it was just a fluke, that it would come soon but another day, and damn, she felt perfectly fine.

By the time the blue dot actually emerged, she'd already known the truth. What she'd spent most of her recent life avoiding like the plague, what she'd mocked other girls for being stupid enough to have happen to them, and what her mother had cautioned her against for what very well may have been literally a thousand times had actually happened to her. And the fact that she'd lived a life doing everything, well almost everything, the "right" way somehow made it even worse.

Yes, Luz was a twenty-year-old honors student in her sophomore year at a prestigious private university. Yes, she'd earned a scholarship and was over a quarter of the way through her English/prelaw major. And yes, "stupid" was the last thing anyone would describe her as. But stupid she was.

Sitting on her bed in her dorm room, the young woman who always knew what to do was at a complete loss. Her mind was racing while her body sat perfectly still. She could hear the constant chatter of voices and chuckles in the hallway and faint music from down the hall and wondered how they could all keep on with their routines. Didn't they know the world was ending?

The first person she told was her roommate Christy, who came in while Luz was still on the bed. Knowing Luz as well as she did, all she could say was, "How did this happen?" This was the question Luz had been repeatedly asking herself since she saw that blue dot.

So she told the story of how, almost two months earlier, she'd done two things she'd never done before and how the first opened the door for the second.

Christy accompanied Luz to the campus health clinic where several things were confirmed: yes, she was pregnant; no, she didn't have any STDs; and, perhaps most significantly, no, she would not even consider having an abortion. She was Catholic, and since she'd been a child it had been drilled into her head with the punishment of an eternity in hell that abortion was a sin, equivalent to murder. Luz was not overly political and would never tell someone else what they could or could not do, but she knew as well as she knew anything that she would not be able to live with herself had she had an abortion.

Luz sleepwalked through the rest of the semester, doing two more things she hadn't ever done before; she earned the first B and first C of her entire academic career. And perhaps even more surprising, she didn't much care. She'd arrived home for winter break petrified at the thought of telling her mother how badly she'd wrecked things.

In contemplating the impending conversation, Luz reflected optimistically on how often the projection of how bad something might be was worse than what it turned out being. However, in this case this particular the axiom was proven false.

Rosemarie screamed until she no longer had a voice. She pounded tables and stomped feet. The small apartment vibrated with the thunderous sounds of rage, frustration, and grief. And upon hearing that the father was essentially missing in action, Rosemarie went over the edge. Doors were slammed and reslammed, cries reverberated, and curses Luz had never even known her mother knew spewed forth. The tirade ended with, "I gave you everything, and you pissed on it…I'm done. If you want to be a nothing, go right ahead. Just don't ask me for help."

Luz fell into a virtually catatonic state. She ate little and slept a lot but did not do much else. She was ashamed to leave the house, to see *anyone* actually. So when winter break was over and it was time to go back for spring, Luz made the decision to stay home—it just seemed like the easiest thing to do.

Luz gave birth to a healthy baby girl she named Jennifer, and the second she saw the child, she was convinced she'd made the right decision. Though she was lighter skinned like her father, her round face and big brown eyes were all Luz. Upon fully taking in the sight of her, Luz did not know she could feel so deeply for another human being and began understanding for the first time why her own mother had been so protective and controlling.

When Rosemarie was first brought in to see the baby, it was as if all of the disappointment and fury she'd had toward Luz melted away. On first sight she too loved the little girl with all her heart.

It had taken a while, but Luz now fully acknowledged that her life had changed at a very fundamental level. She no longer pined to be back at school or was kept from sleeping not only by Jennifer's cries but by the waves of question marks about her future that danced in her head.

With the pregnancy finally over and Jennifer in her arms, she felt an especially revelatory exhale, as if she'd unwittingly been holding her breath ever since the blue dot had materialized, or maybe even before.

Perhaps out of necessity more than anything else, Luz and Rosemarie became a team. In the process of raising Jennifer, Rosemarie taught Luz how to be a mom, and Luz continued to better understand why her mother had done much of what she'd done. Despite the added wild-card variable of raising a child, or perhaps because of it, the two fought less.

Like many parent-child relationships, with Luz now a full adult herself, their relationship shifted from primarily top-down to a much more egalitarian one. With their newfound respect and understanding came new vulnerabilities, which were followed by the inevitabilities of sharing and increased understanding. Having been such a "unique" child, Luz had few friends at home, thus Rosemarie became not only a guide to motherhood but a confidant.

The two talked constantly, discovering much about each other, perhaps most notably how much they did not know. Rosemarie learned how hard it was for Luz to have to constantly live up to expectations, and Luz learned how uncertain Rosemarie was when making decisions about Luz's upbringing. "Like you, motherhood was new to me. I was only a year older than you. I did the best I could, but I do have regrets."

As a means of explaining some of her more extreme parenting practices, Rosemarie shared her vision of Luz pulling them both to the suburbs: "I know you didn't owe me or anything like that, and maybe it *was* selfish, but I wanted that life so badly, for both of us."

With increased familiarity came a closeness neither one of them would have had the audacity to have previously imagined possible.

Just as they were done cleaning up after Jennifer's first-birthday party, and the birthday girl was fast asleep, Rosemarie asked if Luz wanted a cup of tea and if they could talk. The first thing she did was apologize for the vile things she'd said the night Luz had revealed her pregnancy. "A mother should never, no matter what, say those things. I am truly ashamed."

She then said, "Luz, first know that I love you more than anything, and I am *still* proud of you, maybe even more so. You are a *great* mom, a natural at this parenting thing. But unlike me, I think, no, I *know*, you're *more* than that. You have a gift, and I want to see you make the most of it. Not for me, but for you—for you and Jennifer. I know you've been thinking about going back to school, but I want you to *stop thinking* and do. I will watch Jennifer whenever you need it, even if I have to cut down on my hours at the supermarket, rearrange my schedule, whatever. Somehow we'll make it work. But only do it if you really want it—if *you* want it."

Luz was both taken aback and conflicted by her mother's comments. On one hand she truly and deeply appreciated the kind words of encouragement as well as the practical offer of help, but at the same time, she'd wished she still had Jennifer as an excuse not to go back to school. The fact was she no longer saw herself as a student (let alone a future lawyer). She was a mom, a single mom at that, and single moms, especially in her neighborhood, didn't just *decide* to go to college. It just wasn't done, especially with young ones at home. They didn't stay up late and write papers and study for exams. Being a mom, a good one anyway, meant devoting any and all time to caring for their children; that was their role, that's what they committed to when agreeing to have the child. To do anything more was nothing but selfish. *Maybe* they worked if they needed to, but that was not something they *chose* to do, not a *voluntary* act. In Luz's mind it was a matter of choice; you could be a mom or you could be a student, but to be both?

Luz had always prided herself on being a realist and in recent weeks had faced facts. She was not a student anymore, and her future was not a "story yet to be written." Her future was now a known quantity, and that made it more comfortable in a way. She would be like many of the girls in the neighborhood, like her mother, and that would be OK. Not what she dreamed of, not what she really wanted deep down inside, but OK. And given the world as it was, who was she to ask for more? But now her mother was pointing to the door of possibility and saying, "Go ahead. I'll even help you through."

A couple of days later, Luz took Jennifer into a wealthier part of the city to have lunch with Rosemarie at work. After the visit the two went for a stroll through the park and then stopped at a newly constructed playground. There were several moms already there, and one struck up a conversation with Luz. "Oh my god, what a *gorgeous* baby!" the woman exclaimed. "And you are so good with her!" Not knowing what to say, Luz shrugged and responded, "Thanks." The woman continued, "My girl was deported last week, and I know we just met, but might I be able to pry you away from your current family? I see how good you are with her, and we pay pretty well. I bet we could work something out."

Like downloading a large file, it took a while for Luz to get the full message. *Did this woman think I was the babysitter? Oh my god, she did!* "I'm not her babysitter," Luz replied curtly, "I'm her *mother*." It was now the woman's turn to be puzzled. She then said, without even a morsel of embarrassment, "Oh, uh, I guess you won't have time then," and got up and walked away.

During the bus ride home, Luz's fury was percolating. She was irate but not exactly sure why. Gradually it dawned on her. It was the massive assumptions this woman made simply by virtue of looking at Luz. The assumption that Jennifer was not hers, and the assumption that the only reason she'd be in that neighborhood was if she were looking after *someone else's* kid. Not only did she assume all of this, but she was so brazen. She did so in such a seemingly effortless manner, and had the audacity, the cojones, to share her assumptions so casually with such certainty in their accuracy. It was painful to admit, but true nonetheless, that when this woman looked at Luz, all she saw was minimum wage, or perhaps slightly above, help, and that this was the only real reason for Luz's existence on Earth.

Then questions began to flood her consciousness: What would Jennifer see when she looked at her mother? More importantly, what did Luz *want* Jennifer to see when she looked at her, or women like her for that matter? And perhaps most significant, how would who Luz was affect what Jennifer thought was possible for herself?

Luz was fortunate enough to be in a position where she could shape answers to those questions and for the first time felt shame for not doing so. She'd been convinced she knew what good mothers were *supposed* to be and do, and, yes, those thoughts restricted her, but they also provided a sense of comfort. Now she began thinking that perhaps that comfort came at too great a price. But now, looking down into her daughter's cherubic face, Luz knew she was ready to pay.

The urban community college's utilitarian and purely functional design was a far cry from the highly stylized and bucolic setting she'd been in what seemed like a lifetime ago. Upon meeting with an academic advisor and sharing her transcripts, she was immediately placed in a special program for high achieving students from low-income households looking to transfer to four-year colleges.

On the morning of her first day of classes, three back to back, Luz found herself unable to leave Jennifer behind. Of course she'd been apart from her before—to run to the store or to go to the pharmacy to pick up some medication or so her mother could take her out and show her off to her friends, but rarely for hours. And never for the five hours of class time she had ahead of her.

Hearing Luz's sobs Rosemarie walked into the room. Luz shared her fears and suggested putting off school for another semester, or maybe a year: "Yeah, I should be ready in a year or so."

"No, mi amor," Rosemarie began. "You will not be ready in a year. You'll want another year then…you will never be *ready* to leave your baby behind, and that's what makes you a great mother. But you have to go back to school, and you will. You'll leave her behind because you love her, and right now going back to school is what's best for you *and* her, and that's why you'll go and do what you've always done—be the smartest kid in the class."

Luz recommitted to school with the same ferocity she'd practiced most of her life, taking more than a full load of courses. But clearly things were different. Even with her mother's help, quiet study time was rare and thus at a premium. She could no longer map out her time down to the minute because her time was no longer fully hers. Study time did not begin at eight o'clock at night; it began when Jennifer happened to fall asleep. The research paper could not be done when Luz was ready; it waited impatiently for Jennifer's fever to subside. Luz could not even shower when she wanted. The loss of control over her time was an ever-present frustration, but Luz never used it as an excuse.

Some of the instructors were highly empathetic, telling her she could bring her daughter to class if absolutely necessary. Others forbade children in class, voicing concerns over disruptions and the inconveniencing of the other students. Luz took advantage of those professors who allowed children and made certain to find other arrangements for those who didn't. She reminded herself that it was *her* decision to have Jennifer, and that it was not the world's job to accommodate that decision.

Though relatively undemanding, having a little human being almost completely dependent on her made managing the community college course work a challenge. A challenge that necessitated more effort and energy than anything she'd done before. However, she'd emerged a year after she began, having completed an associate's degree in English, earning a 4.0 grade point average in the process.

Having been accepted to the honors program there, she was to begin what was essentially her junior year at an elite public university a manageable forty-five minute commute from her home. At the honors program's orientation, the faculty emphasized how much work would be required, particularly for English and history majors. "Get ready to live at the library," the hunched over, gray haired professor quipped.

Upon returning home Luz relayed to her mother the professors' warnings. She talked about all of the research and papers and time at the library and again suggested some possible time off, but all Rosemarie said was, "No, mi amor."

So back to school she went—her third college in as many years. During that first semester, she realized two things: the hunched, gray haired professor was not a liar, and, perhaps more importantly, school was school and classes were classes, and though the assignments were more time-consuming and demanding, the same habits and strategies, though amped up a bit, that worked before would work again.

While her time was still not fully her own, in many ways Luz was a better student now than she'd been before. The hard fought maturity and perspective she'd gained over the past years provided her with both a sense of gratitude for the opportunity to spend time learning and an enhanced appreciation for the learning itself. Rather than just working to get the A, the knowledge and ideas themselves became equally valuable. These changes in focus ingratiated her to her professors who would routinely describe both her and her papers as "evolved," "wise," and "well balanced."

By the time Jennifer was talking in complete sentences, Luz was beginning her senior year of college and had amassed an array of effective academic strategies as well as valuable human resources she could draw upon when necessary. She felt a sense of awareness, assuredness, and competence that went well beyond anything she'd experienced prior to Jennifer's birth. It was as if she'd uncovered a part of herself that was missing but had been there all the time.

Often she'd run into friends from high school she hadn't seen in a while, and when they'd sometimes ask, "Are you in school? Have any kids?" Luz would reply, with a smile, "Yes."

You Work It

You may want to spend some time analyzing specifically *how* Roger and Luz worked the formula. In doing so you'll probably realize that while there were some common themes, they went about their resilience in very different ways. Certain steps in the formula may have been more significant for one than the other. That's OK—that's life. Neither Roger, Luz, you, nor I are rats in a study, responding to stimuli in the same exact ways. We are messy, inconsistent, unpolished, and often unpredictable. We are human. And to quote Carl, "It's OK, man, it really is."

If you are currently in the midst of a major life crisis, I strongly recommend you use this book and the formula as one of your tools in the process of bouncing back.

Briefly restated—

- Honestly and objectively assess what has occurred, ditching both the rose-colored glasses and the doom and gloom.
- Cultivate meanings regarding the event that are both truthful and empowering, and attach what it is you find most important to overcoming the crisis.

- Design a strategic plan you believe in deeply and go about the process of implementing it.

Finally, as you hit any of the proverbial roadblocks that will surely dot your path back from whatever trauma you face, remember that you are *built to be resilient.* The machinery of resilience literally and figuratively courses through your veins, and what's more, it *longs for* and *craves* expression. Whether it's our bodies' immune systems, our minds' defense mechanisms, or our souls' spirits, we *yearn* for healing, for a return to homeostatic equilibrium. Appreciating and celebrating our resilient natures helps us muster the courage and patience necessary to both reveal that nature and manifest its wonder.

A LETTER TO THE READER

Dear Reader,

My measure of a book like this has always been the answer to the following: Did I get at least three quality ideas from its reading? My sincerest hope is that you can answer a resounding yes! However, keep in mind that ideas are often only as valuable as what we do with them, thus we cannot underestimate the significance of mustering the courage to act in accordance with these newly formed attitudes. As Henry David Thoreau famously wrote, "Live your beliefs and you can turn the world around."

Thank you for taking the time to read this. I welcome any feedback, reactions, or experiences.

If you would like to learn more about resilience you may visit my website, www.livingresilience101.com, or email me directly at docmorales@comcast.net.

Best,

Erik Morales

August 20, 2013, Jersey City, NJ

REFERENCES

Chapter I: Resilience IOI

1. Goleman, D. 1995. *Emotional Intelligence*. New York: Bantam Books.
2. Tough, P. 2012. *How Children Succeed: Grit, Curiosity, and the Hidden Power of Character*. Boston: Houghton Mifflin.
3. Garmenzy, N. 1991. "Resiliency and vulnerability to adverse developmental outcomes associated with poverty." *American Behavioral Scientist* 34 (4): 416–430.
4. Rutter, M. 1979. "Protective Factors in Children's Responses to Stress and Disadvantage." *Primary Prevention of Psychopathology, 3: Social Competence in Children*. Hanover: University Press of New England.
5. Werner, E. and R. Smith. 1992. *Overcoming the Odds: High Risk Children from Birth to Adulthood*. New York: Cornell University Press.
6. Gilbert, D. 2006. *Stumbling on Happiness*. New York: Knopf.
7. Seligman, M. 2011. *Flourish: A Visionary New Understanding of Happiness and Well-being*. New York: Free Press.
8. Peterson, C. 2006. *A Primer in Positive Psychology*. New York: Oxford.
9. Dwek, C. 2006. *Mindset: The New Psychology of Success*. New York: Ballantine Books.

Chapter 2: Acceptance

1. Gardner, H. 1983. *Frames of Mind: The Theory of Multiple Intelligences*. New York: Basic Books.
2. Pronin, E. 2008. "How We See Ourselves and How We See Other." *Science* 320: 1177–1180.

3. Davidveale, A., et. al. 1996. "Body Dysmorphic Disorder: A Survey of Fifty Cases." *British Journal of Psychiatry* 169: 196–201.

4. Morales, E. and F. Trotman. 2008. *A Focus on Hope: Fifty Resilient Students Speak.* Rowman Littlefield/University Press.

5. Gordon, Larry and Louis Sahagun. 2007. "Gen Y's Ego Trip Takes a Bad Turn: A New Report Suggests that an Overdose of Self-esteem in College Students Could Mean a Rough Road Ahead." *Los Angeles Times,* February 27.

6. Dweck, C. 2007. "The Perils and Promise of Praise" *Early Intervention at Every Age.* 65 (2): 34–39.

7. Fox, M. 2010. "Personal Conflicts Biggest Cause of Murders in U.S." Reuters, 5/13/2010*Reuters, 5/13/2010.* Fox, M. (2010). *Reuters, 5/13/2010.*

8. Goleman, D. 1995. *Emotional Intelligence.* New York: Bantam Books.

9. Mackillop, K. 2011. "The Real Ego Risks of Entrepreneurship." *Wisepreneur.* http://wisepreneur.com/entrepreneurship/the-real-ego-risks-of-entrepreneurship.

10. Suzuki, S. 1970. *Zen Mind, Beginner's Mind.* New York: Weatherhill.

Chapter 3: Meaning

1. Frankl, V. 1959. *Man's Search for Meaning.* New York: Washington Square Press.

2. Ruiz, D.M. 1997. *The Four Agreements.* San Rafael: Amber–Allen Publishing.

3. Wolin, S. and S. Wolin. 1993. *The Resilient Self: How Survivors of Troubled Families Rise Above Adversity.* New York: Villard Books.

4. Burroughs, A. 2012. *This Is How.* New York: St. Martin's Press.

5. Twenge, J., B. Gentile, N. DeWall, D. Mad, K. Lacefield, and D. Schurtz. 2010. "Birth Cohort Increases in Psychopathology

Among Young Americans, 1938–2007: A Cross-Temporal Meta-analysis of the MMP." *Clinical Psychology Review* 30: 145–154.

6. Waterman, A. 2005. "When Effort Is Enjoyed: Two Studies of Intrinsic Motivation for Personally Salient Activities." *Motivation and Emotion* 29 (3): 165–188.

7. Ryan, R. and E. Deci. 2011. "A Self-Determination Theory Perspective on Social, Institutional, Cultural, and Economic Supports for Autonomy and Their Importance for Well-Being." *Cross Cultural Advancements in Positive Psychology* 1(1): 45–64.

8. Buchholz, T. 2011. *Rush: Why You Need and Love the Rat Race.* New York: Hudson Street Press.

9. Brown, D. 2012. "Does Life Need Meaning? CSU Tackles Ultimate Query." *The Denver Post,* January 17 (Web posting).

10. Weinstein, N. and R.M. Ryan. 2010. "When Helping Helps: Autonomous Motivation for Prosocial Behavior and Its Influence on Well-being for the Helper and Recipient." *Journal of Personality and Social Psychology* 98: 222–244.

11. Bunderson, I. and J. Thompson. 2009. "The Call of the Wild: Zookeepers, Callings, and the Double-edged Sword of Deeply Meaningful Work." *Administrative Science Quarterly* 54 (1): 32–57.

12. Towers Perin. 2012. *www.Workawesome.com/career/true-calling.* Accessed June 3.

13. Wrzesniewski, A., C. McCauley, P. Rozin, and B. Schwartz. 1997. "Jobs, Careers, and Callings: People's Relations to Their Work." *Journal of Research in Personality* 31: 21–33.

14. Murray, M. http://www.sharecare.com/question/purposeful-life-orientation-important-health. Accessed March 7, 2012.

15. Bennett, D. L. Barnes, A. Buchman, and P. Boyle. 2010. "Effect of a Purpose in Life on Risk of Incident Alzheimer Disease and Mild Cognitive Impairment in Community-Dwelling Older." *General Psychiatry* 67(3): 304–310.

16. Fiore, K. 2010. "Living a Purposeful Life Can Stave Off Alzheimer's" *MedPage Today* http://abcnews.go.com/Health/AlzheimersNews/purpose-life-stave-off alzheimers /story?id=9986018. Accessed May 2, 2012.

17. Novak, D. 2011. "Stress, Challenge and the Rat Race" http://blogs.wttw.com/moreonthestory /2011/05/10/stress-challenge-and-the-rat-race/. Retrieved May 13, 2012.

Chapter 4: Action

1. Bandura, A. 1977. "Self-efficacy: Toward a Unifying Theory of Behavioral Change." *Psychological Review* 84 (2): 191–215.

2. Rotter, J. 1966. "Generalized experiences for internal versus external control of reinforcement." *Psychological Monograph* (80): 609–809.

3. Poll, Marcist. 2011. "It's Destiny! Most Americans Believe in Soul Mates." http://maristpoll.marist.edu/210-its-destiny-most-americans-believe-in-soul-mates. Accessed July 17, 2012.

4. Reyes, C. 2011. "When Children Fail in School: Understanding Learned Helplessness." http://educationforthe21stcentury.org/2011/02/when-children-fail-in-school-understanding-learned-helplessness/ Accessed November 11, 2012.

5. Jones, E. and R. Nisbitt. 1972. *Attribution: Perceiving Causes of Behavior.* Morristown: General Learning.

6. Veiga, A. 2012. "Average US Credit Card Debt Per Borrower up in 3Q." *Bloomberg BusinessWeek* News. November 19.

7. US Department of Commerce, Bureau of the Census. 2005. "Money Incomes of Households, Families, and Persons in the United States," Income, Poverty, and Valuation of Noncash Benefits" Current Population Reports, Series P-60. *Digest of Educational Statistics.*

8. Mischel, W., Y. Shoda, and M. Rodriguez. 1989. "Delay of Gratification in Children." *Science* 244 (4097): 933–938.

9. Lakein, A. 1974. *How to Get Control of Your Time and Your Life.* New York: Signet.

10. Hardy, D. 2010. *The Compound Effect: Multiplying Your Success One Simple Step at a Time.* New York: Vanguard Press.

Chapter 5: Returning to the Spring: Identifying, Using, and Valuing Our Personal Charging Stations

1. Moore, T. 1992. *Care of the Soul: A Guide for Cultivating Depth and Sacredness in Everyday Life.* New York: Harper Collins.

2. Dowling, S. 2005. "Images in psychiatry, George Engel, M.D. (1913–1999)." *American Journal of Psychiatry* 162 (2039).

3. Cameron, D. 2010. "Placebos Work—Even without Deception." *Harvard Gazette* (December).

4. Csikszentmihalyi, M. 2009. *Flow: The Psychology of Optimal Experience.* New York: Harper Collins.

5. Center's Forum on Religion & Public Life http://www.patheos.com/blogs/friendlyatheist /2012/03/29/what-percentage-of-prisoners-are-atheists-pew-forum-offers-an-answer/. Accessed April 16, 2012.

6. Federal Bureau of Prisons Statistics. 1997. http://www.bop.gov. Accessed April 16, 2012.

7. Koenig, H. 200). *Handbook of Religion and Health.* New York: Oxford University Press.

8. Allen, C. 2003. "The Benefits of Meditation." *Psychology Today.* April 1.

9. Gardner, H. 1983. *Frames of Mind: The Theory of Multiple Intelligences.* New York: Basic Books.

10. National Health Service. http://www.nhs.uk/Conditions/ Seasonal-affective-disorder/Pages/Causes.aspx. Accessed April 17, 2012.

11. Landers, D. 1997. "The Influence of Exercise on Mental Health." *PCFS Research Digest* 2 (12).

12. Surrenda, D. 2012. "The Purpose of Yoga." *New York Times Op-Ed,* January 12.

13. Anders, M. 2005. "Does Yoga Really Do the Body Good?" *ACE Fitness Matters,* (September/October).

14. Kiecolt-Glaser, J.K, et al. 2010. "Stress, Inflammation, and Yoga Practice." *Journal of Biobehavioral Medicine* 72 (2), 113–121.

15. Pope, V.T. and W.B. Kline. 1999. "The Personal Characteristics of Effective Counselor: What Ten Experts Think." *Psychological Reports* 84: 1339–1344.

16. Ponton, L. 2006. "Characteristics of Effective Counseling." *Psych Central.* http://psychcentral.com/lib/2006/characteristics-of-effective-counseling/ Retrieved on April 25, 2012.

17. Giles, L. et al. 2005. "Effects of Social Networks on 10 Year Survival in Very Old Australians: The Australian Longitudinal Study of Aging." *Journal of Epidemiol Community Health* 59: 574–579.

18. Pope, T. P. 2009. "What Are Friends For: A Longer Life." *New York Times* April 20.

19. "Jack Needs Jill to Get Up the Hill." 2009. *University of Virginia Magazine.* (Fall).

20. Pavlina, S. 2008. *Personal Development for Smart People.* New York: Hay House, Inc.

Made in the USA
Charleston, SC
19 September 2013